In Loving Memory

Churchyard

Adult Coloring Book

by

Tabz Jones

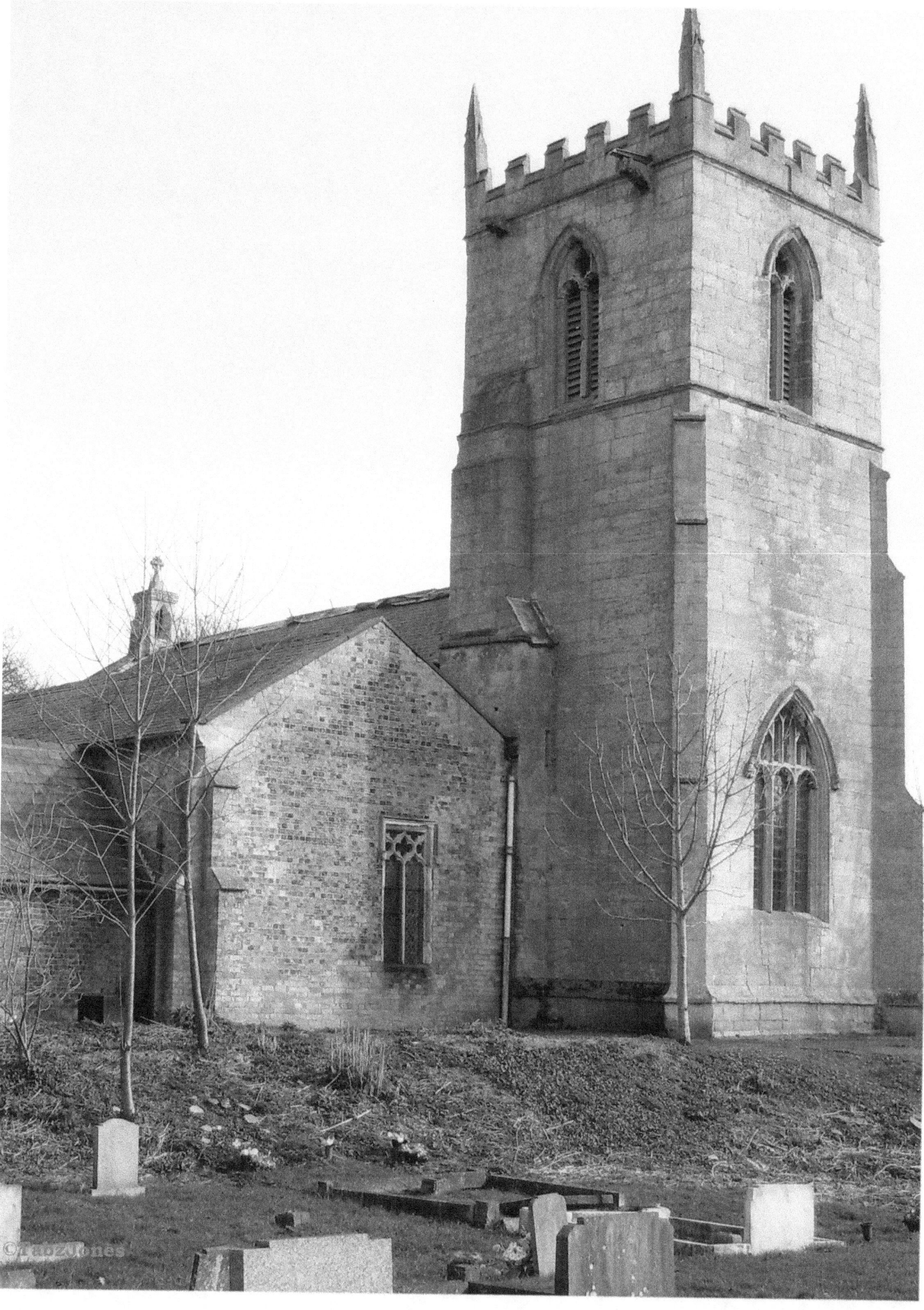

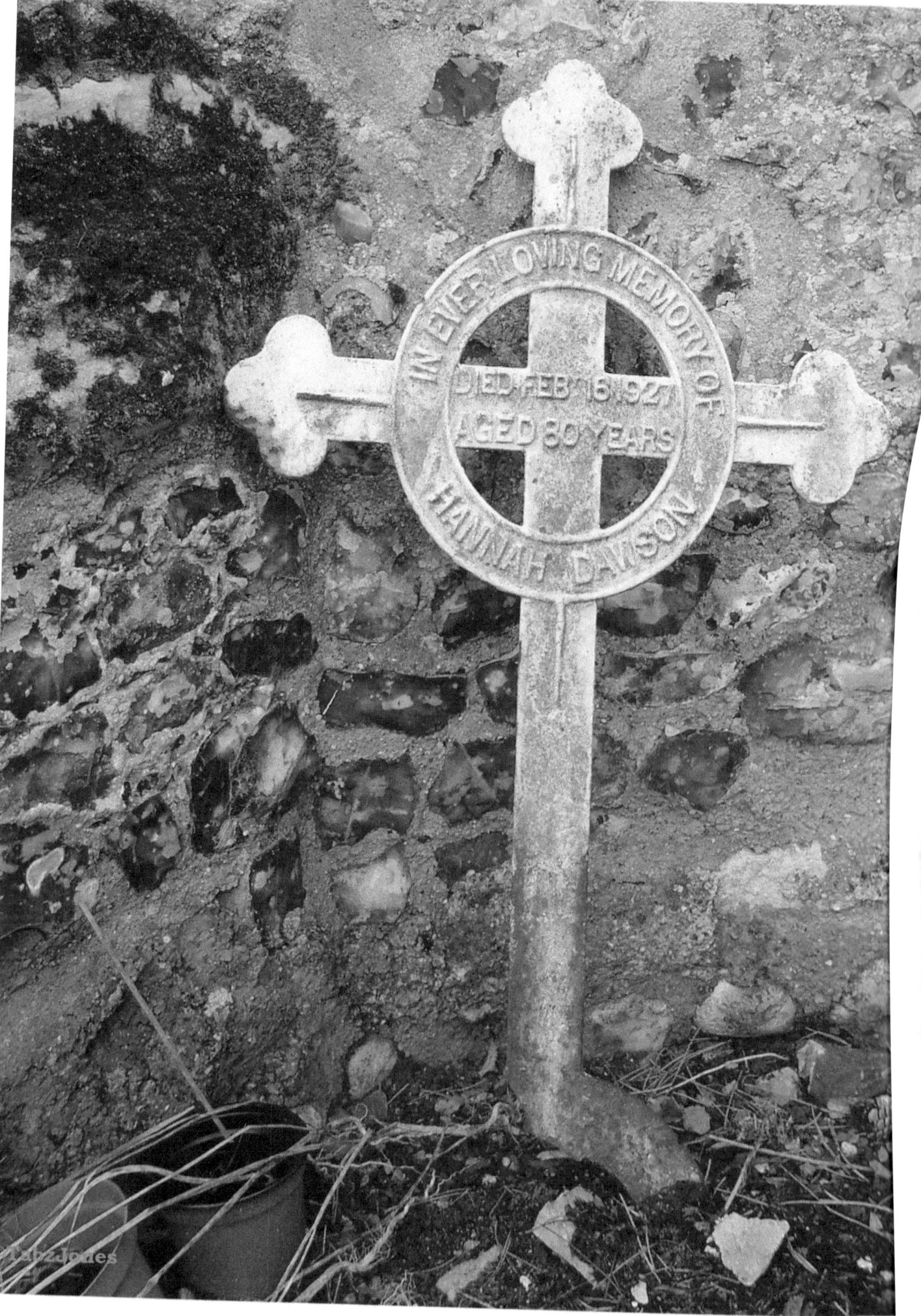

IN EVER LOVING MEMORY OF
DIED FEB 16 1927
AGED 80 YEARS
HANNAH DAWSON

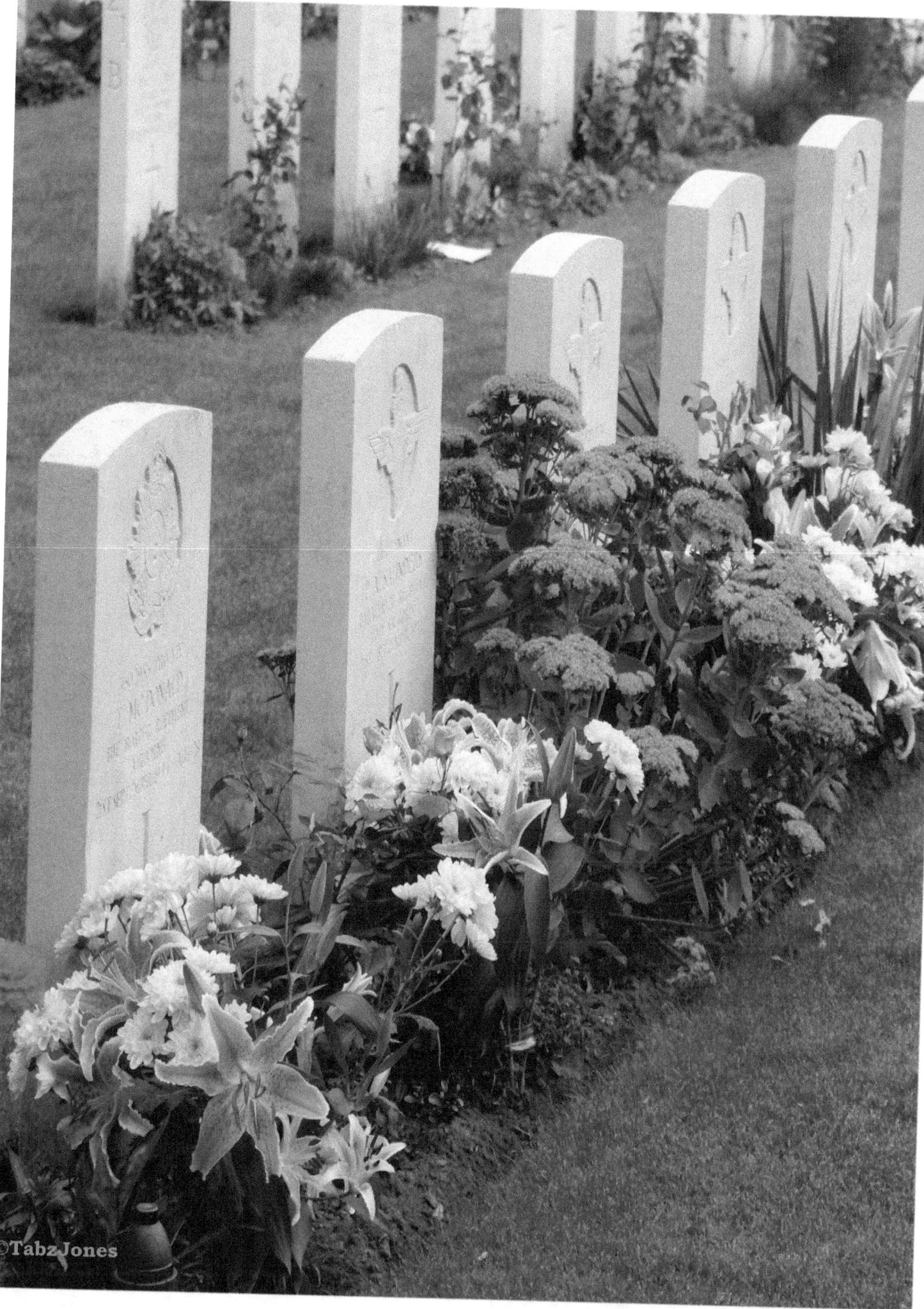

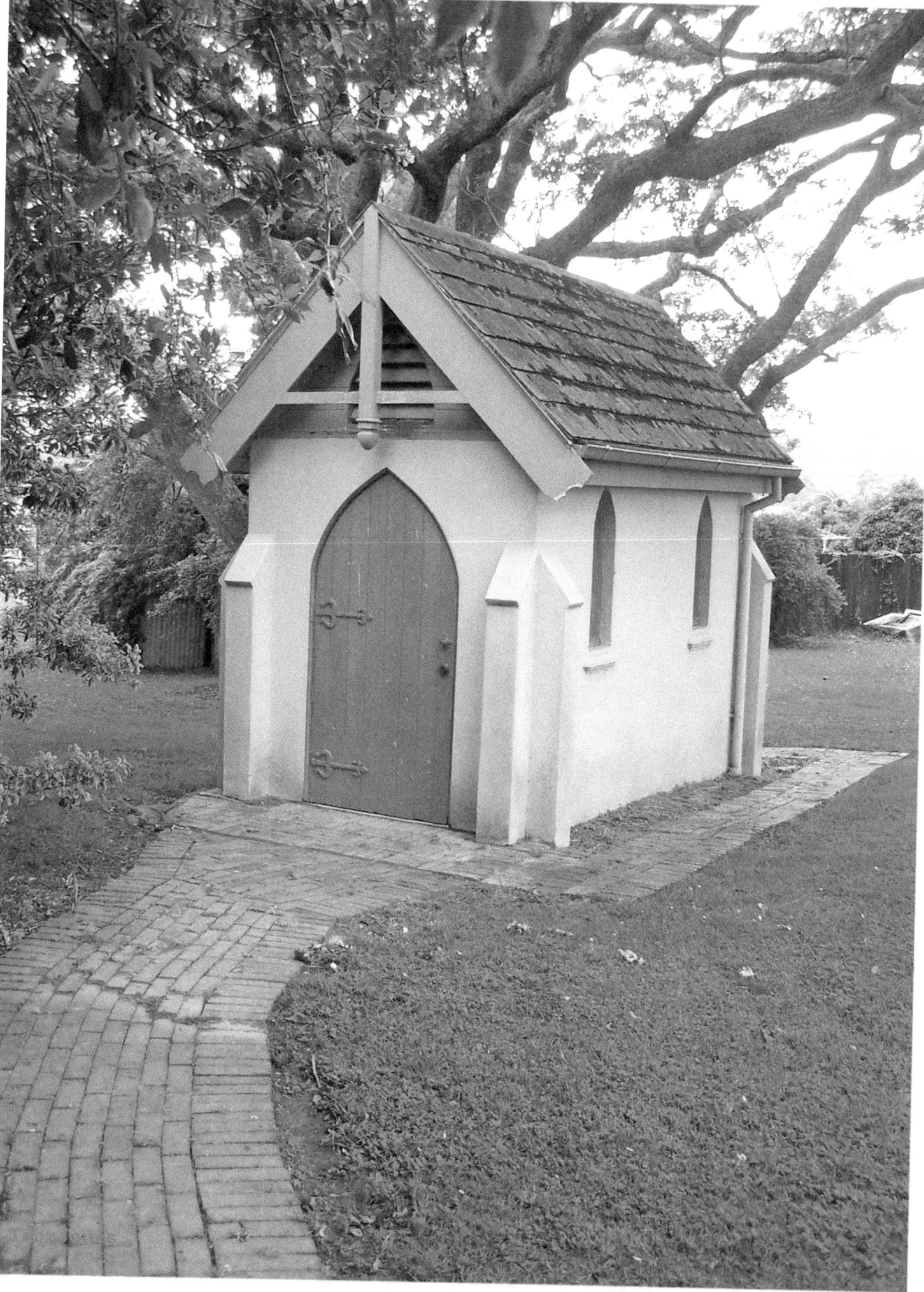

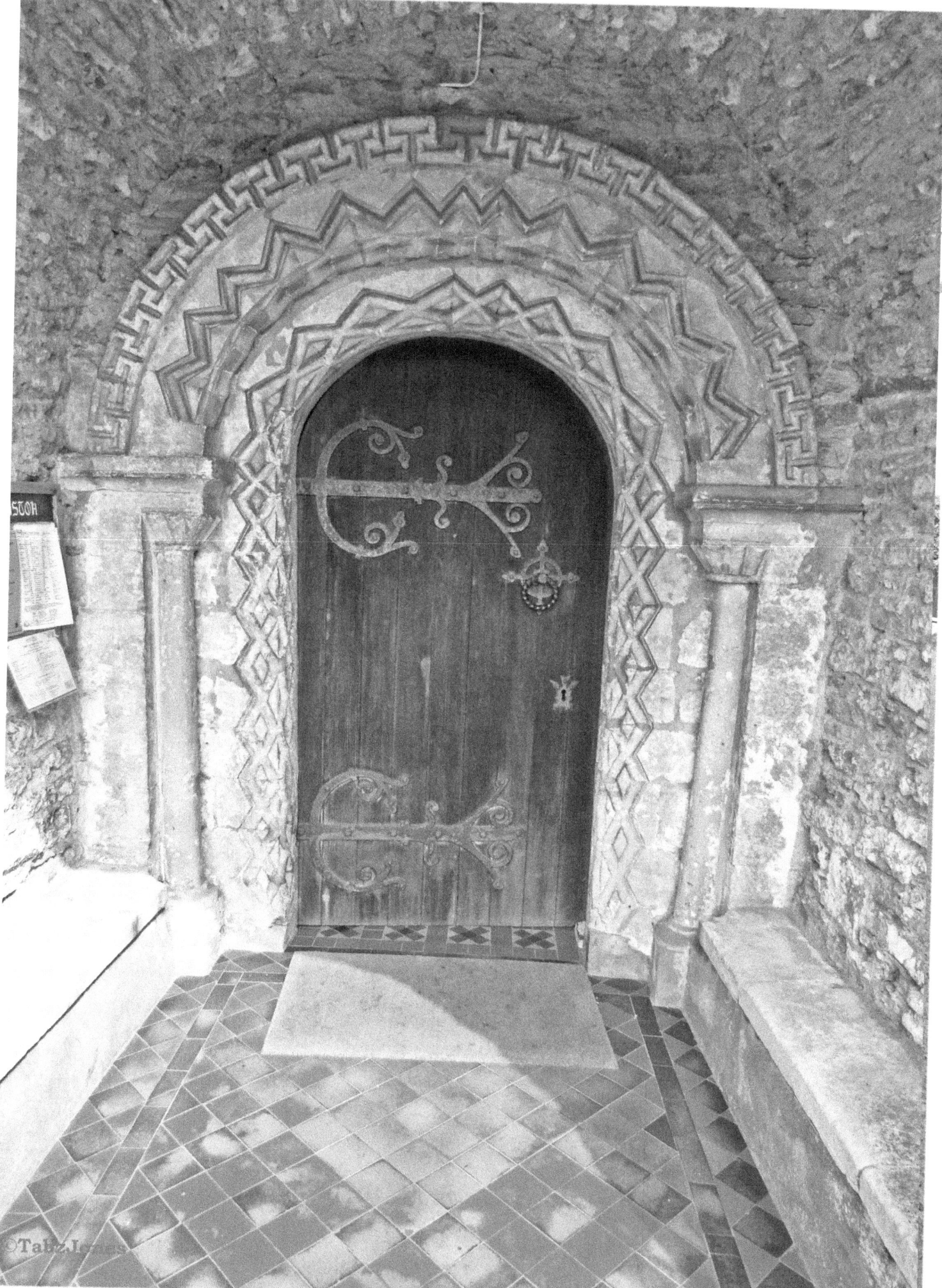

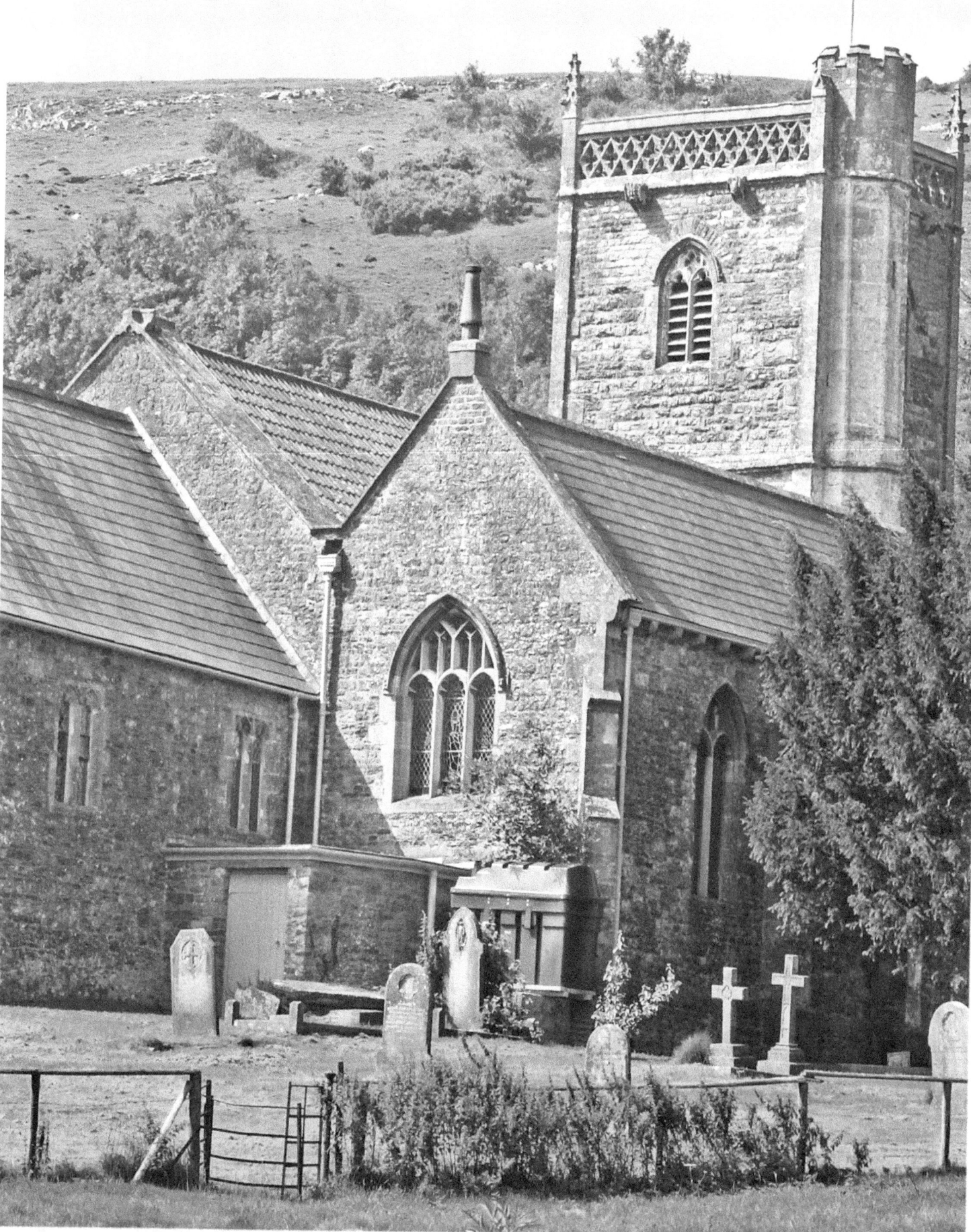

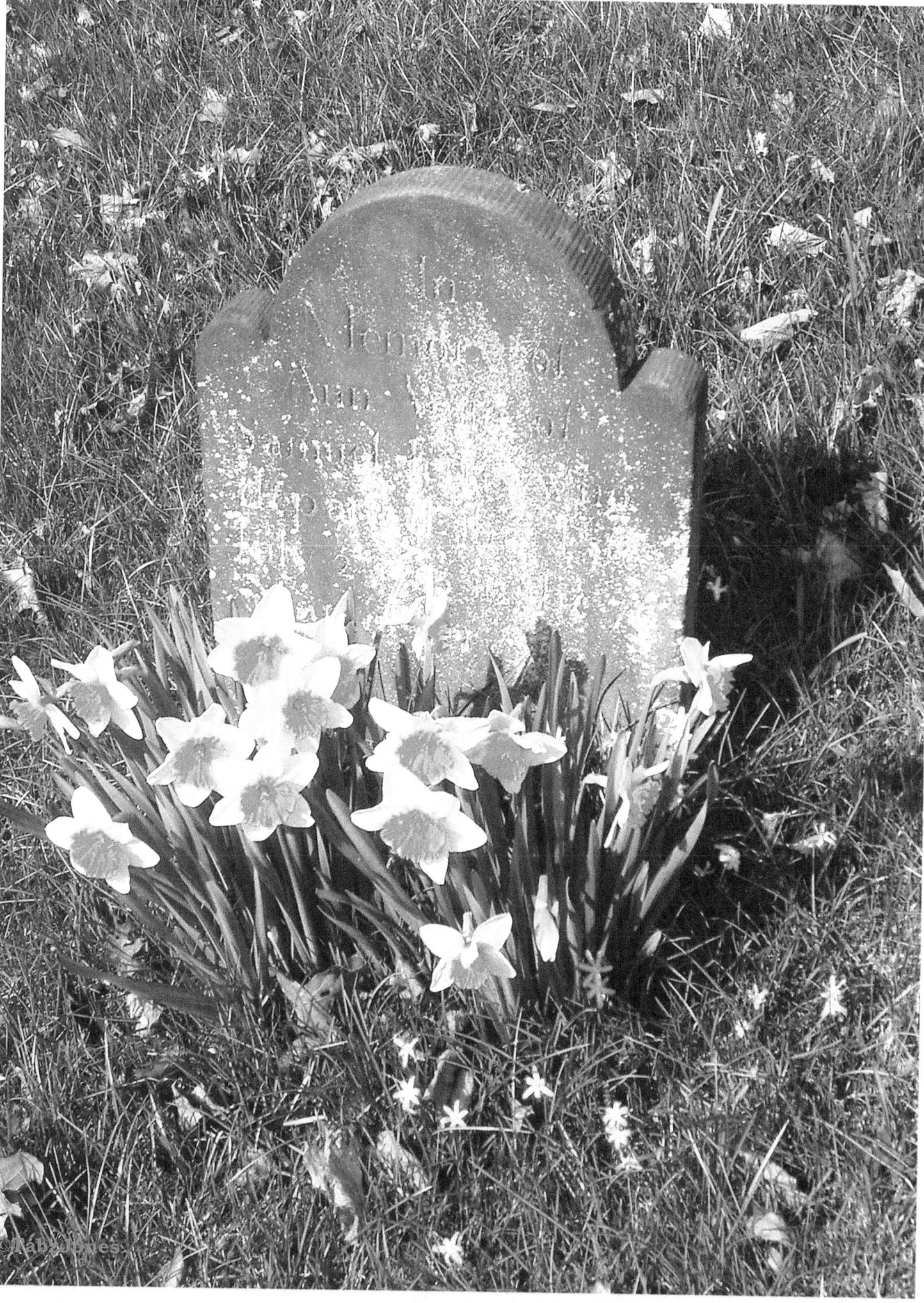

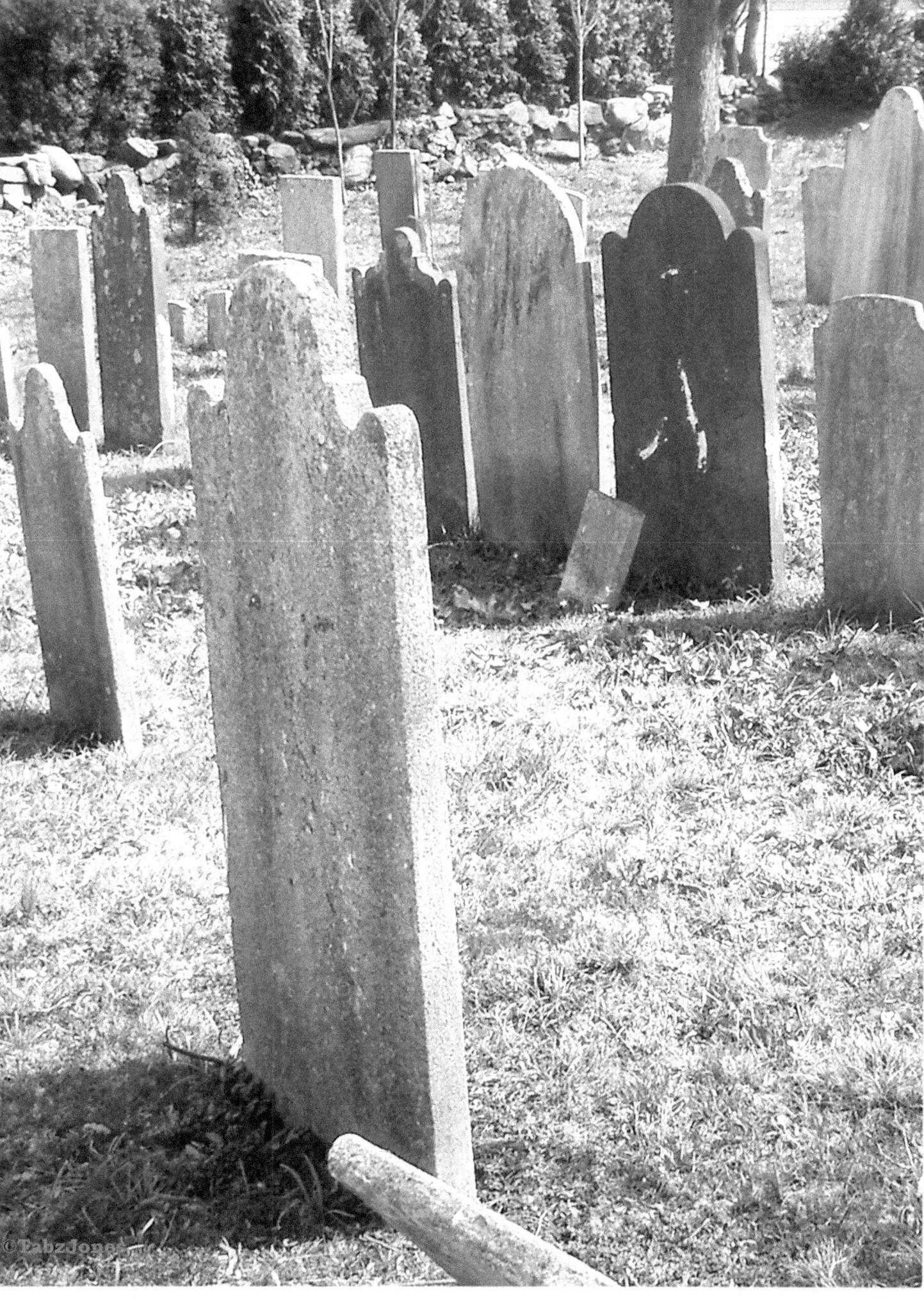
©PabzJones

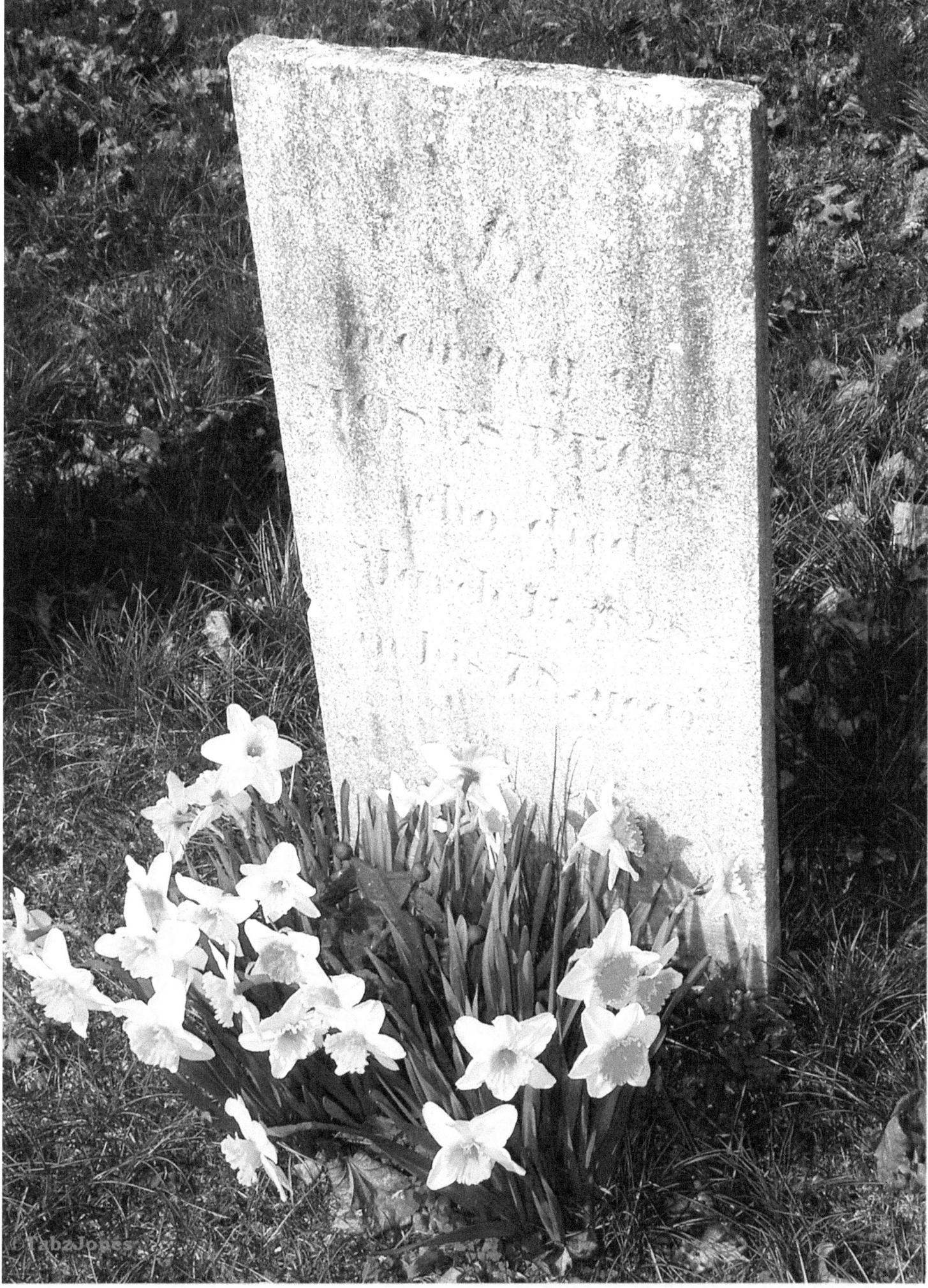

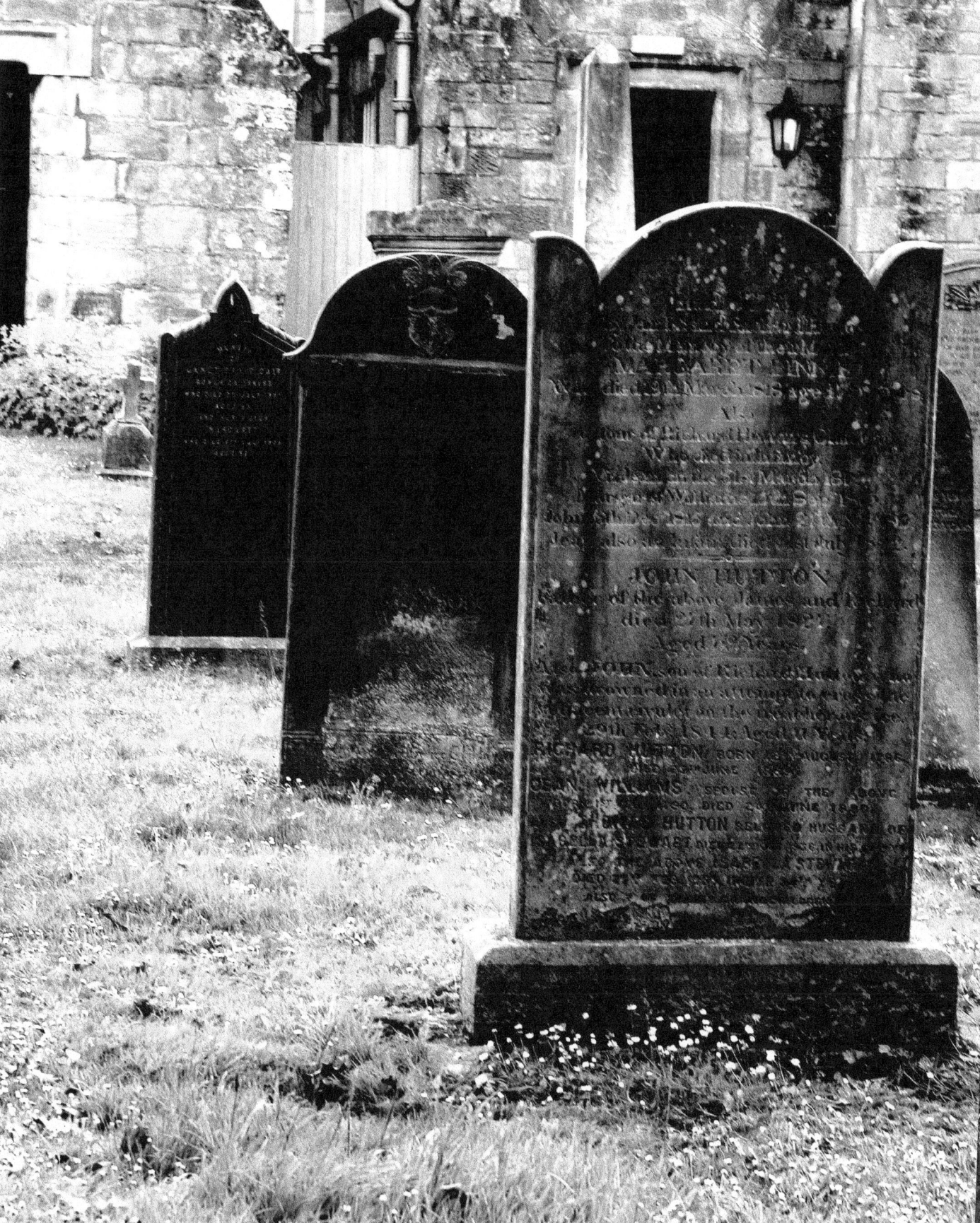

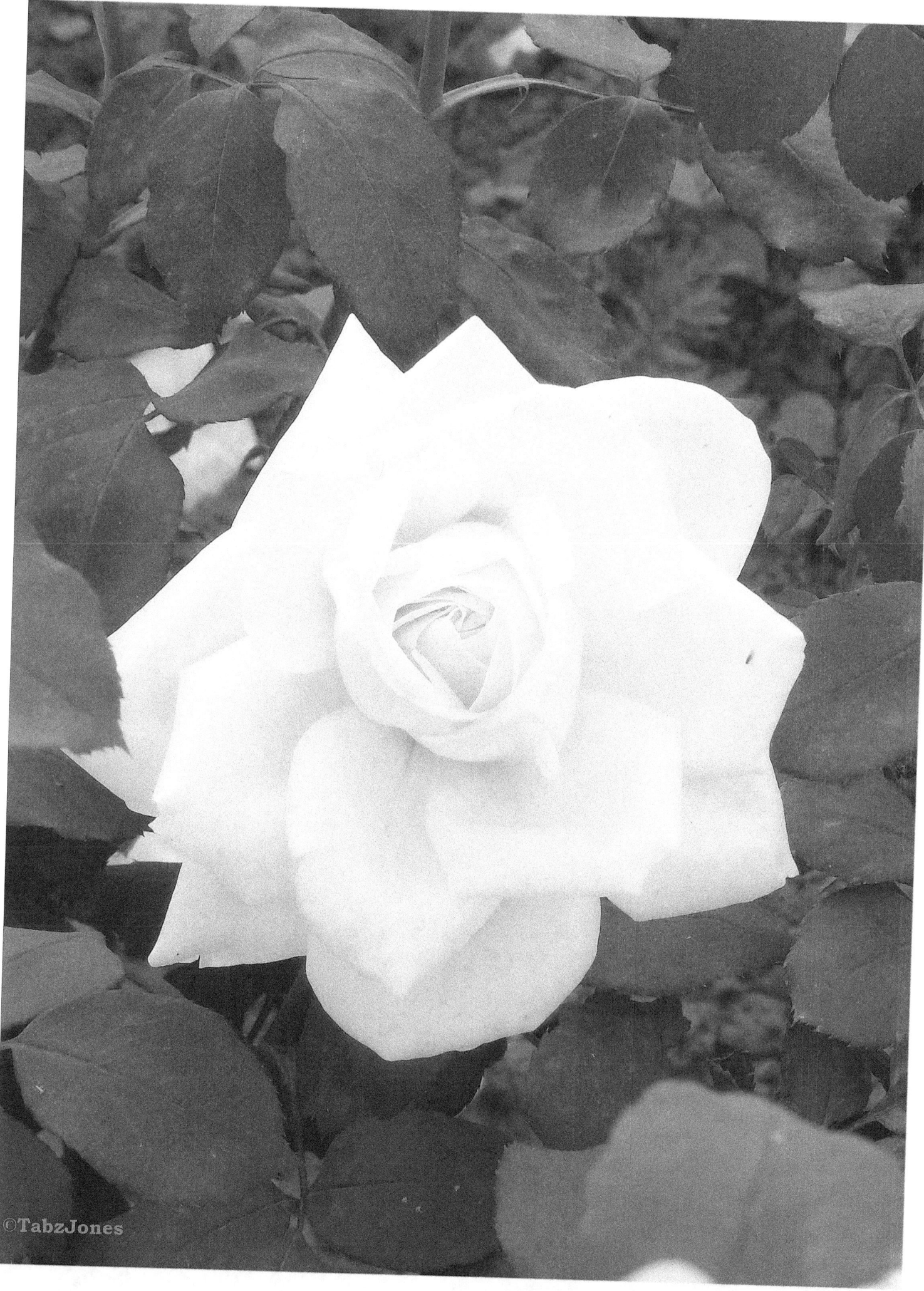

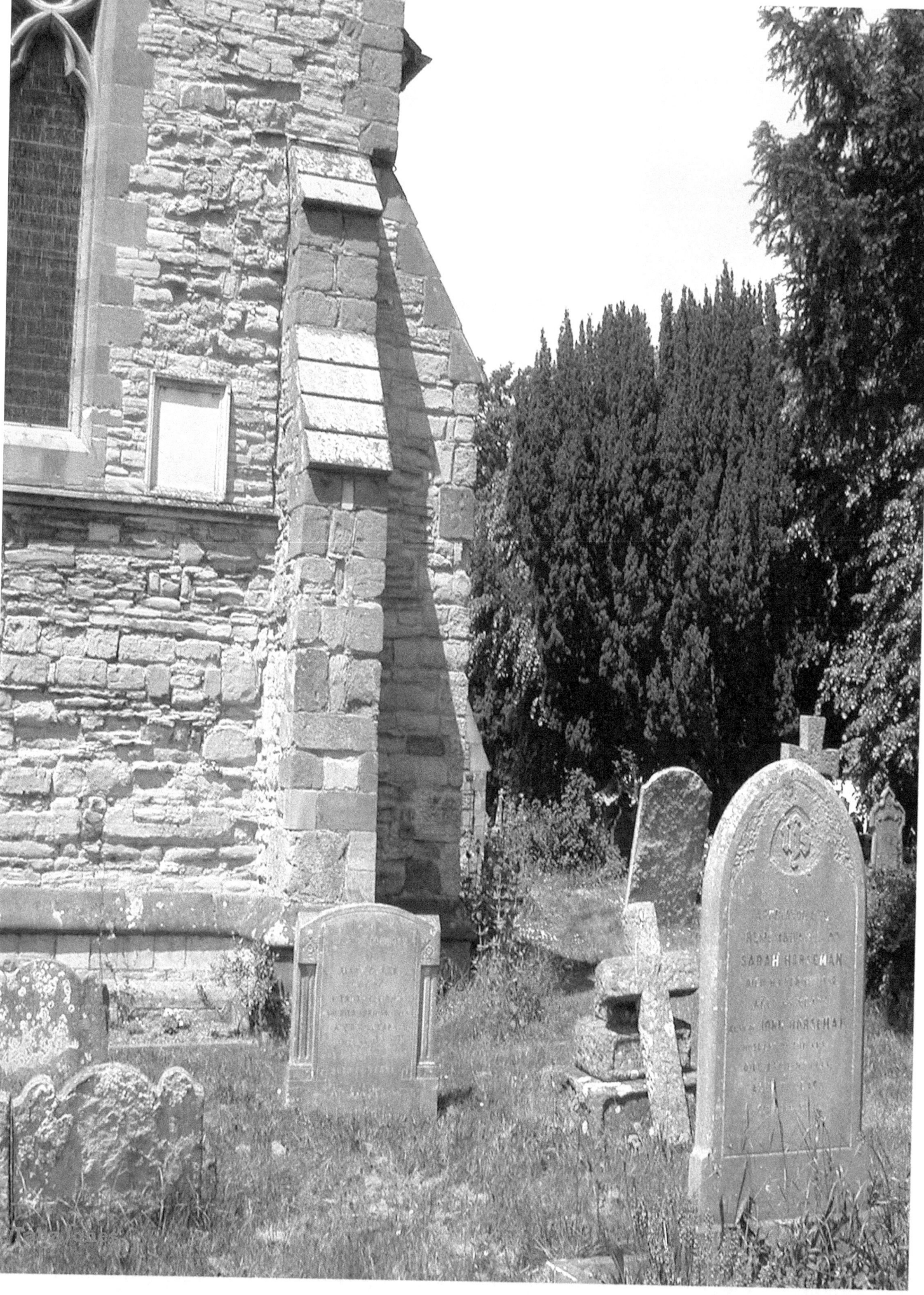

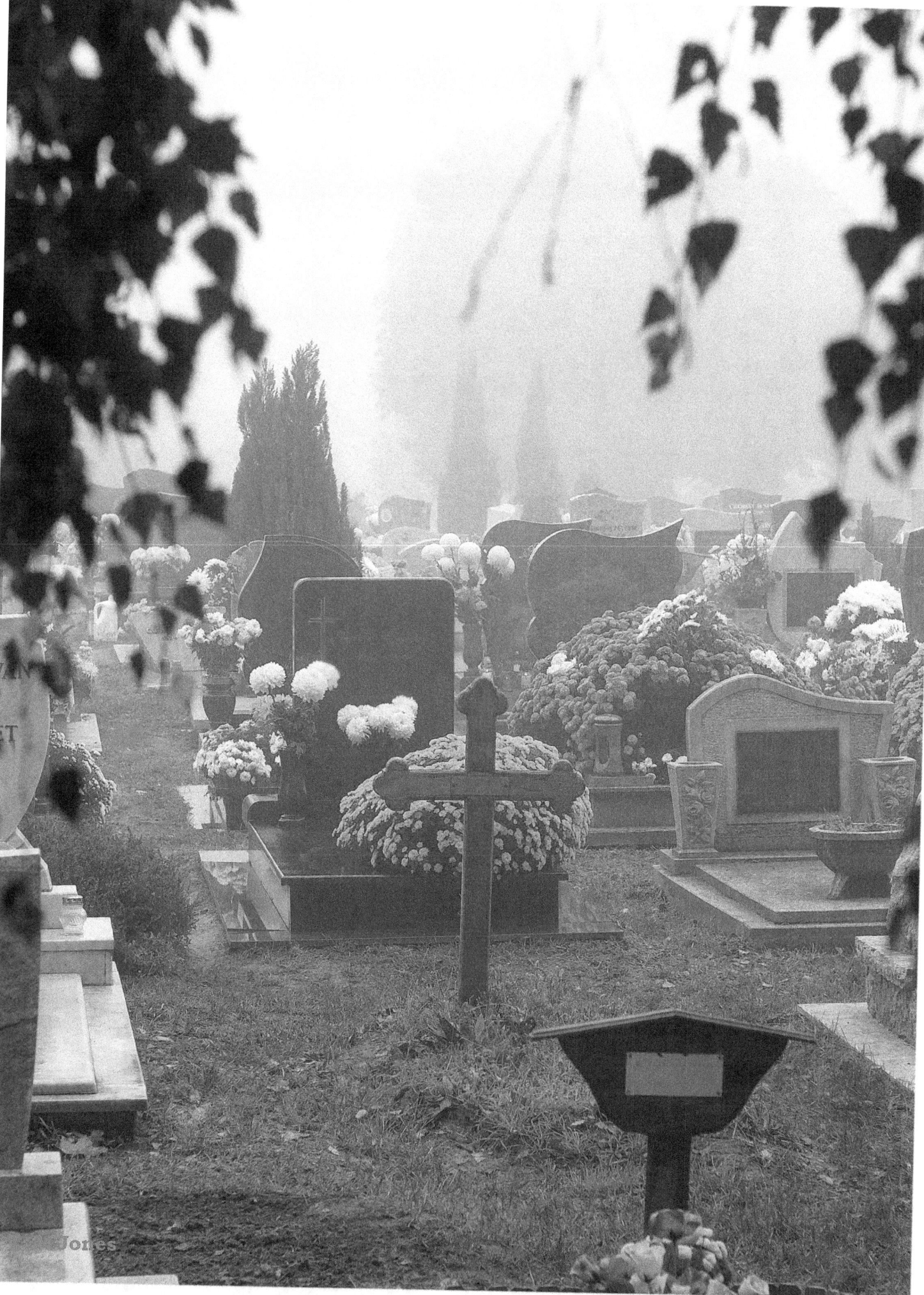

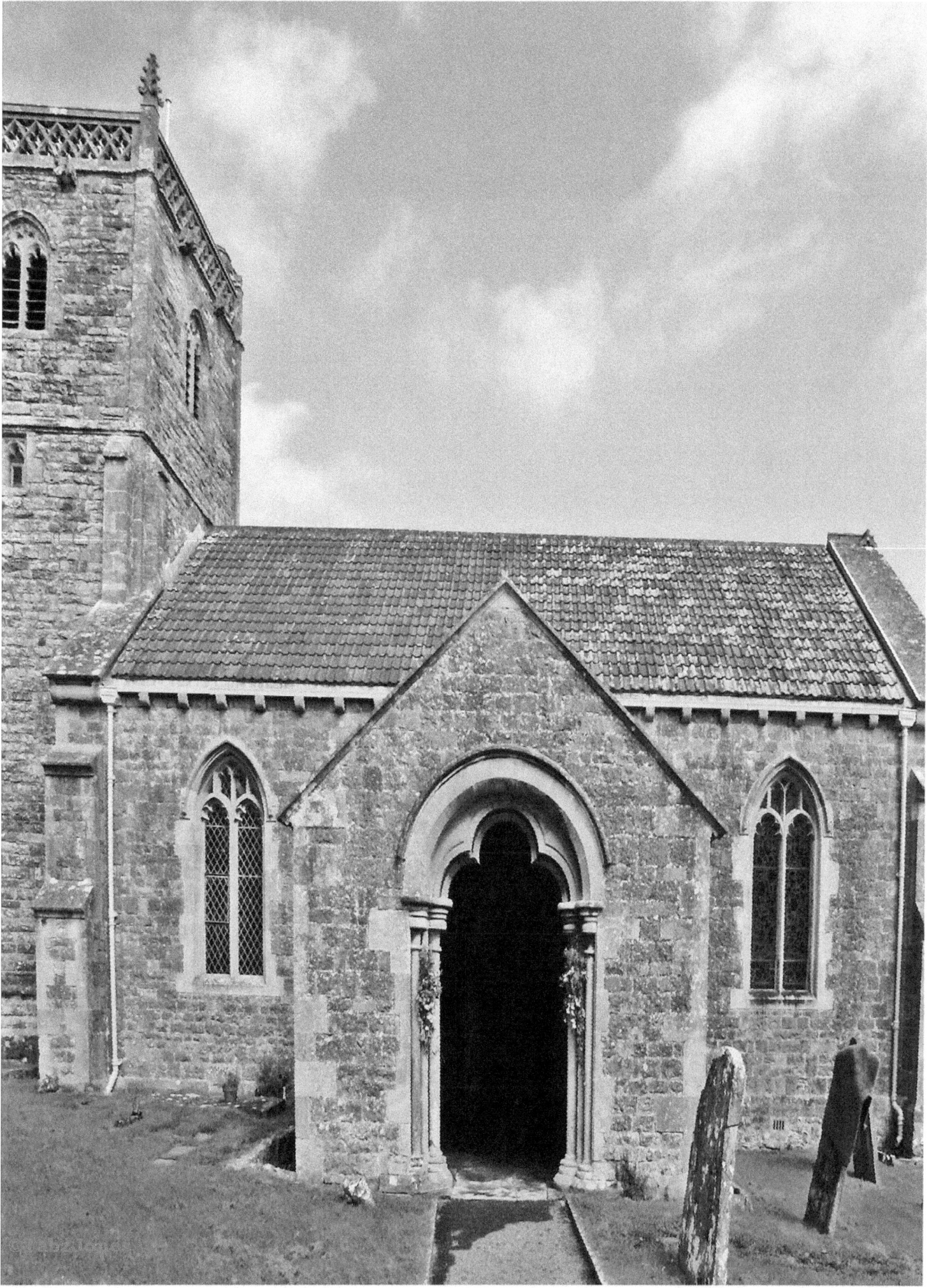

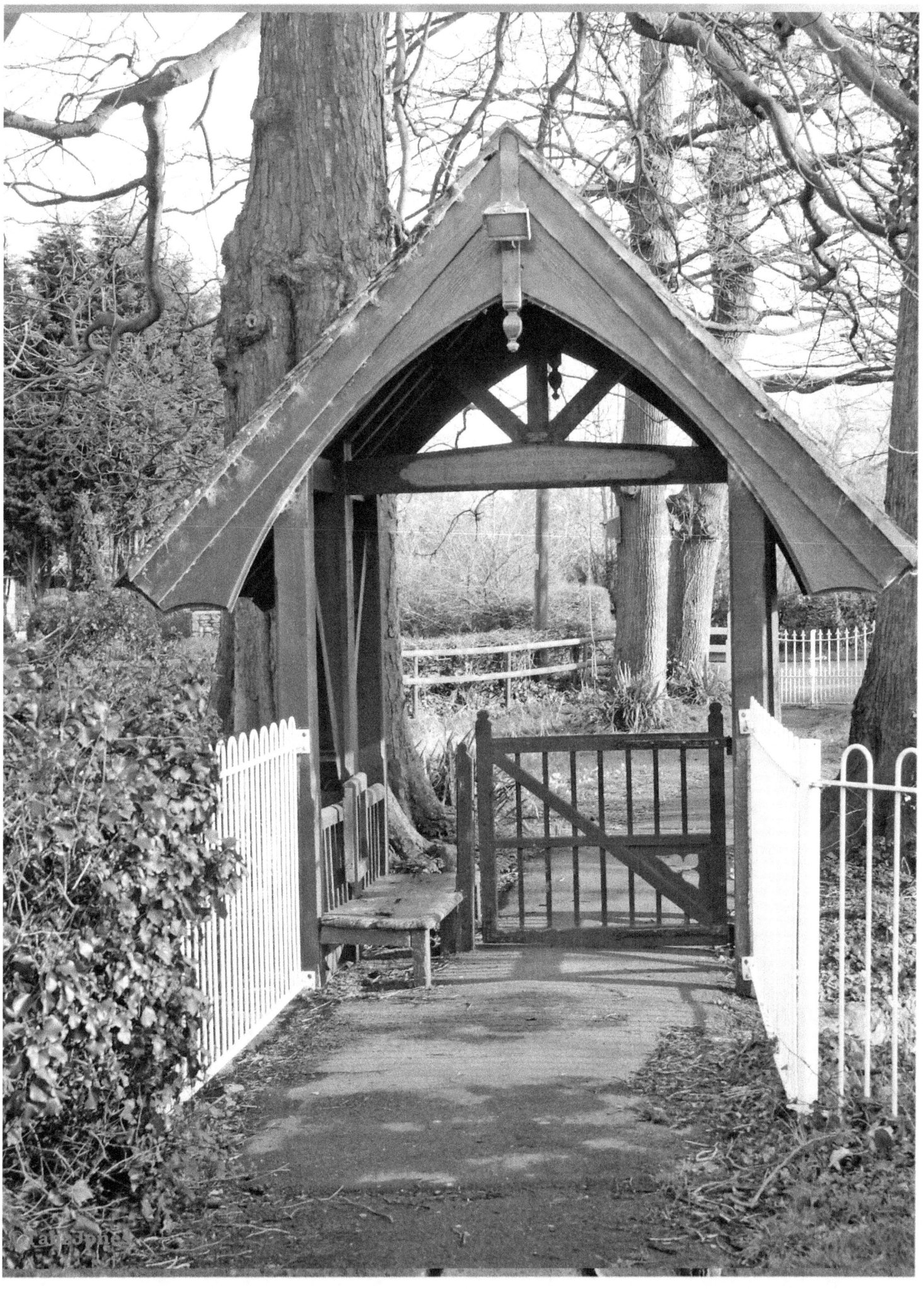

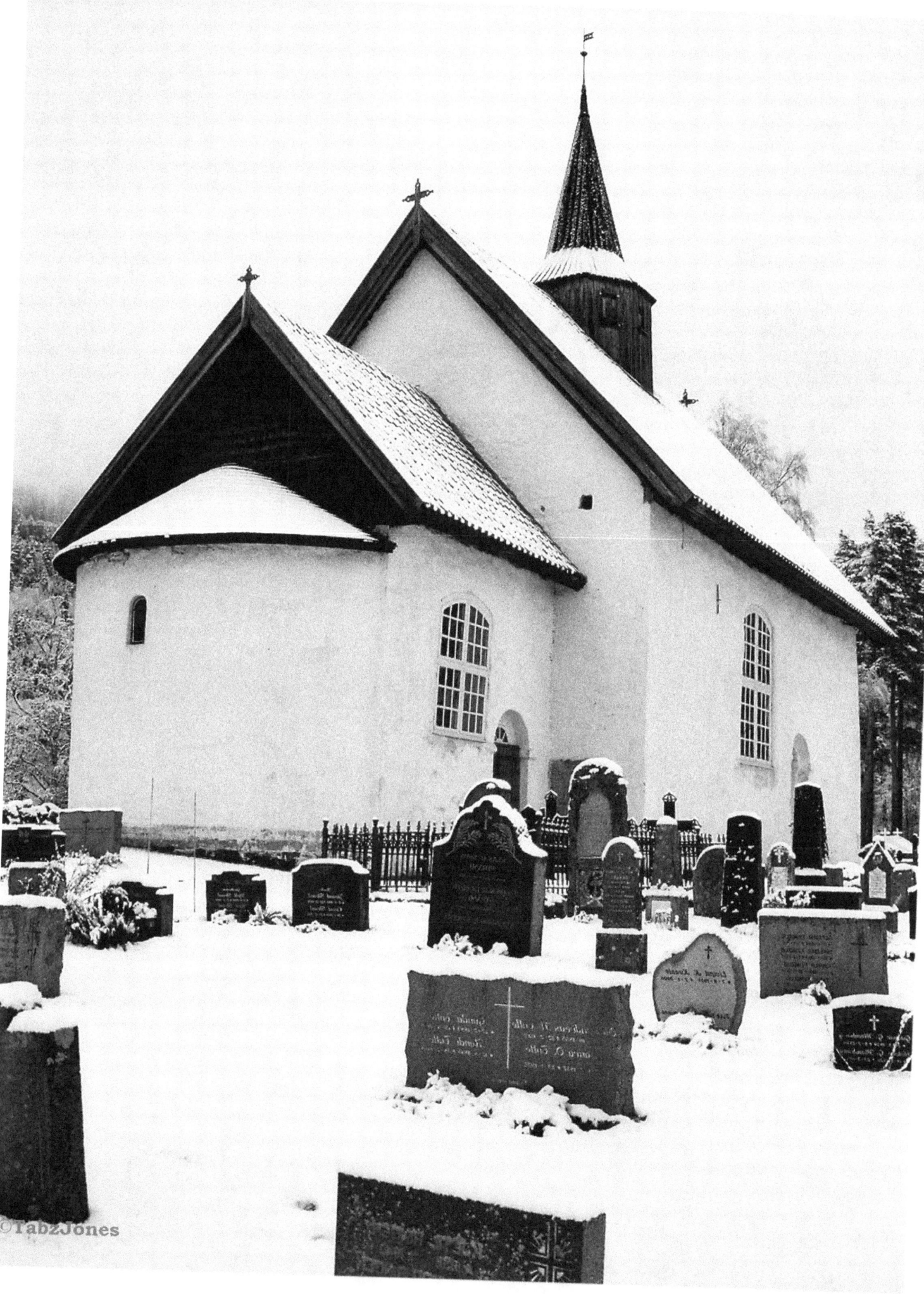
©Tab2Jones

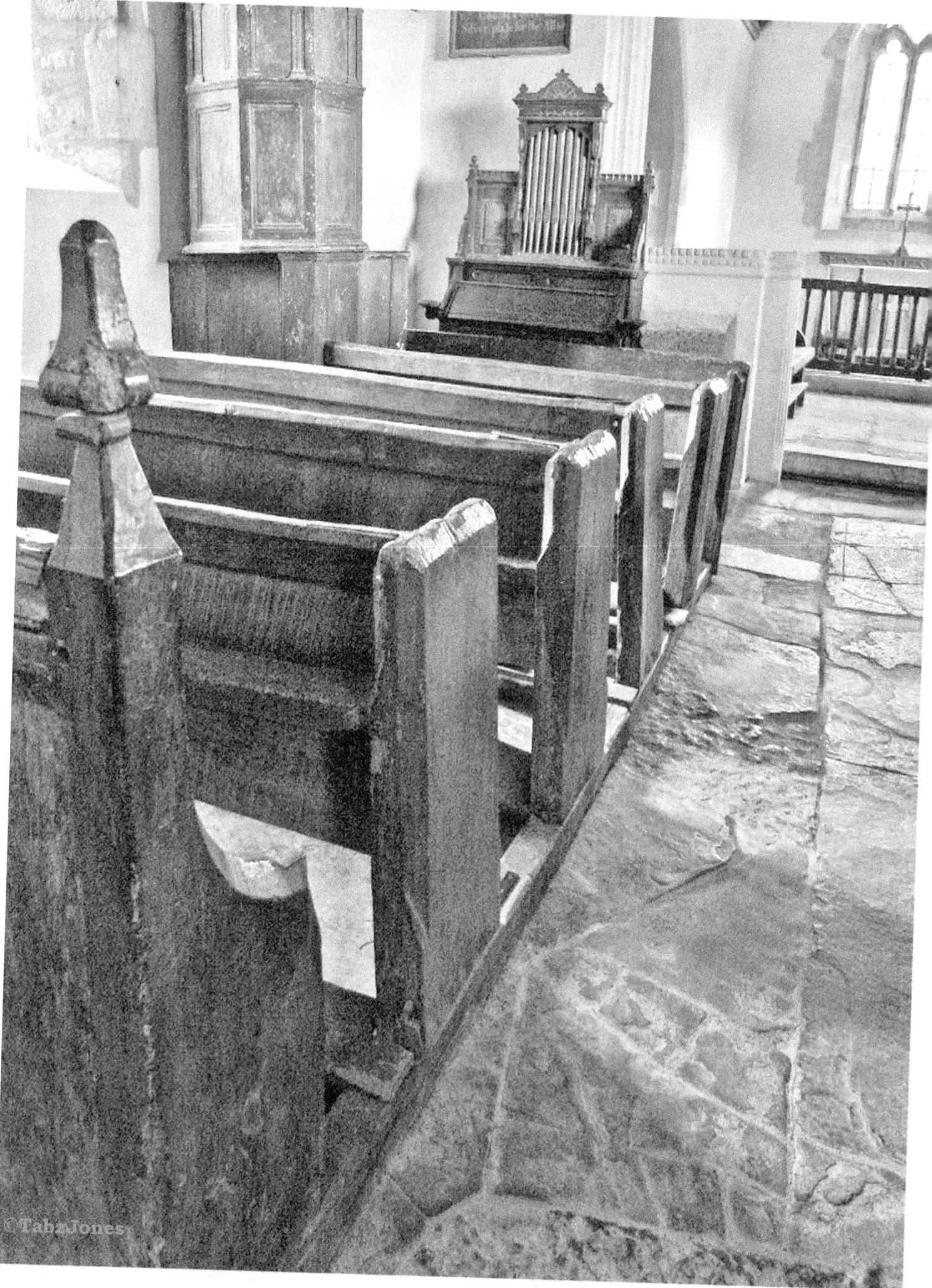

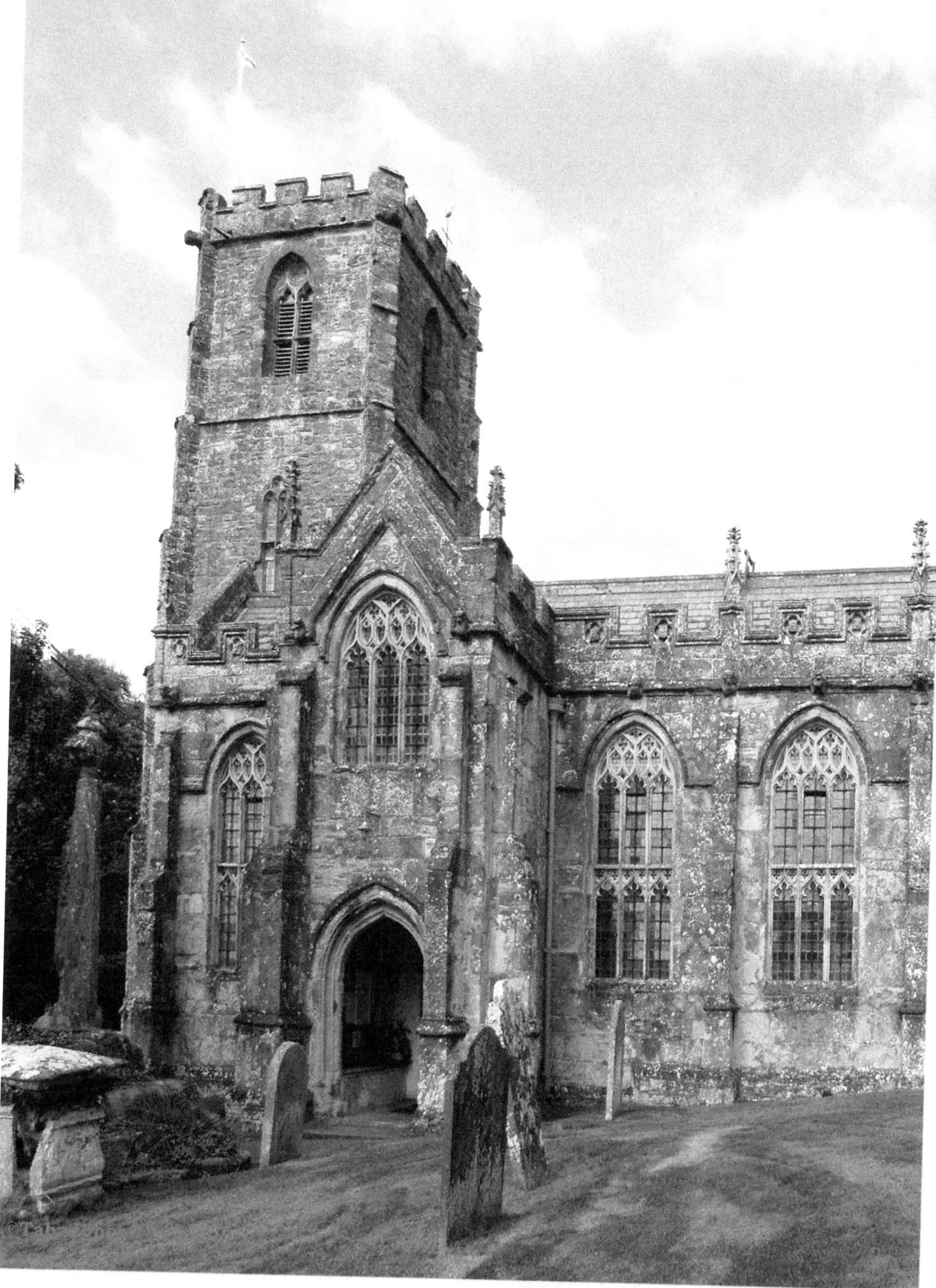

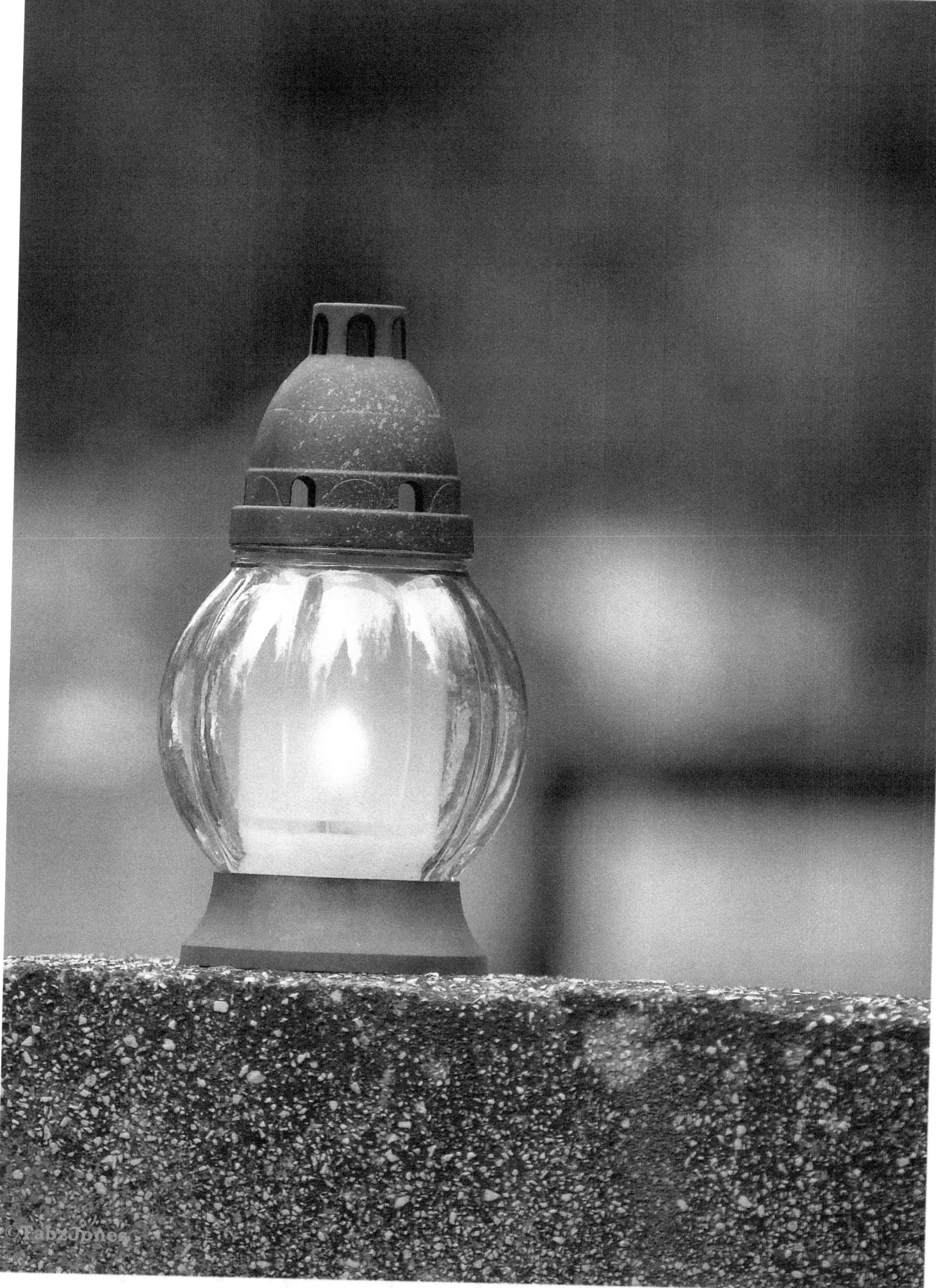

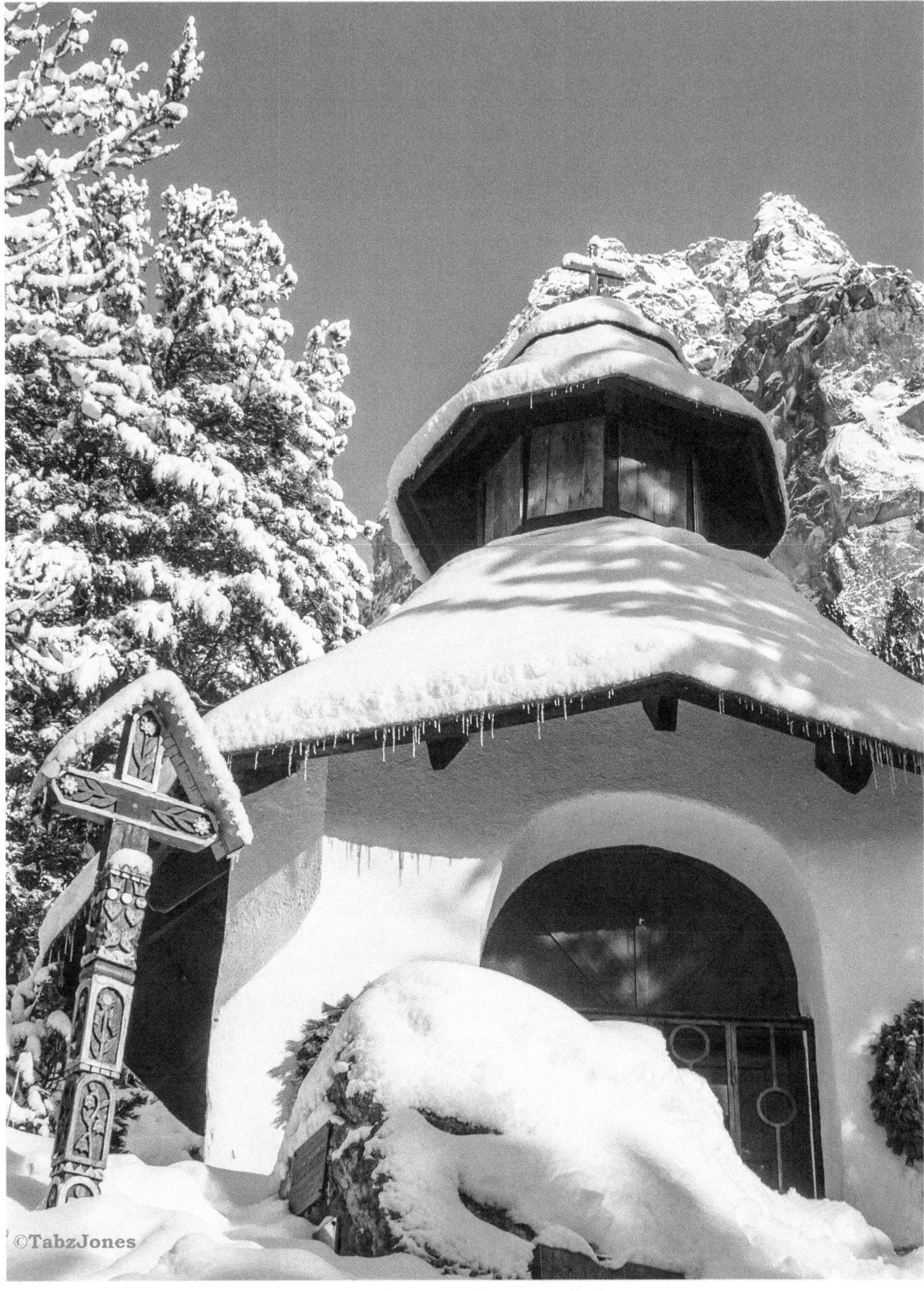

©TabzJones

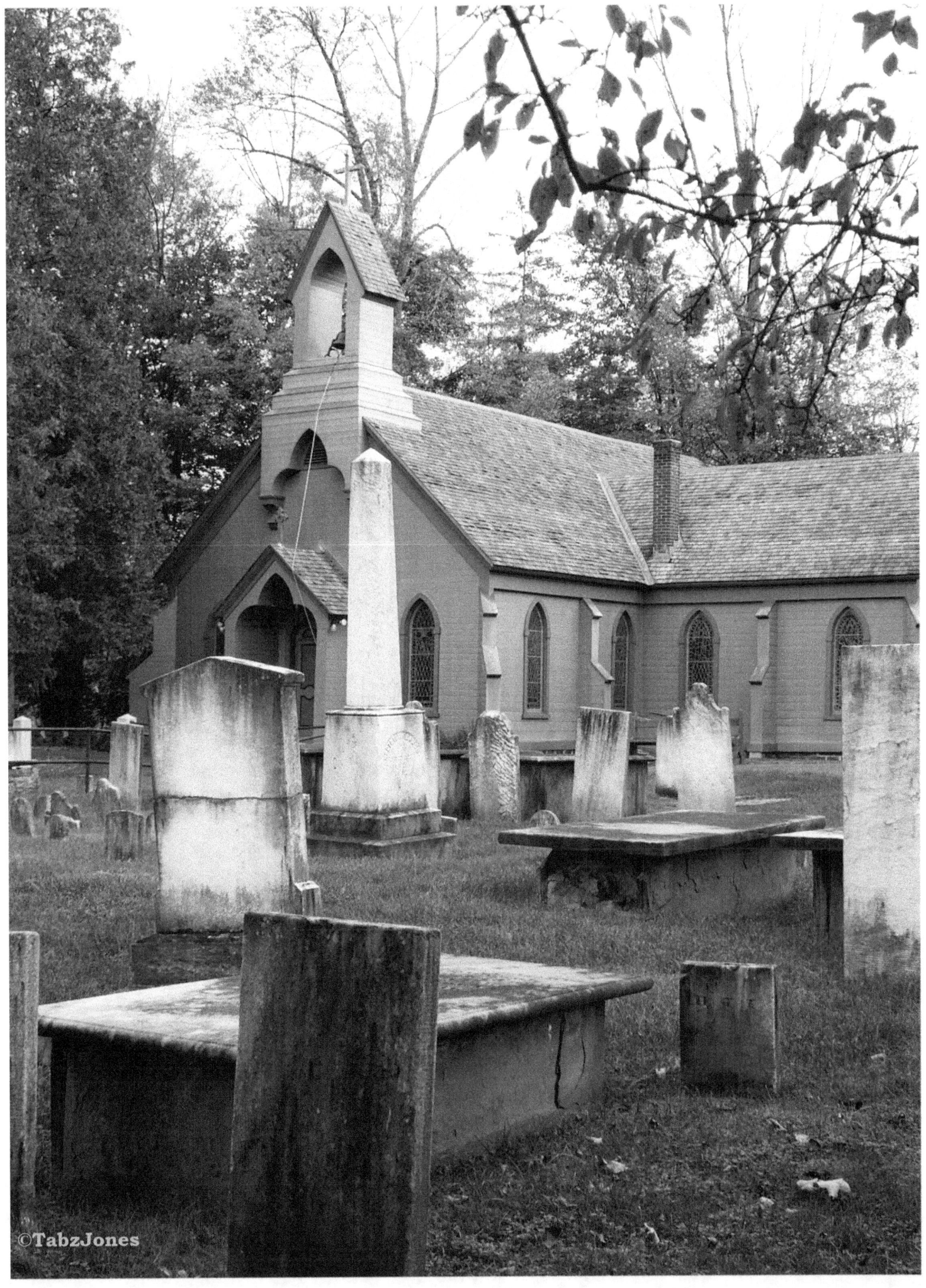

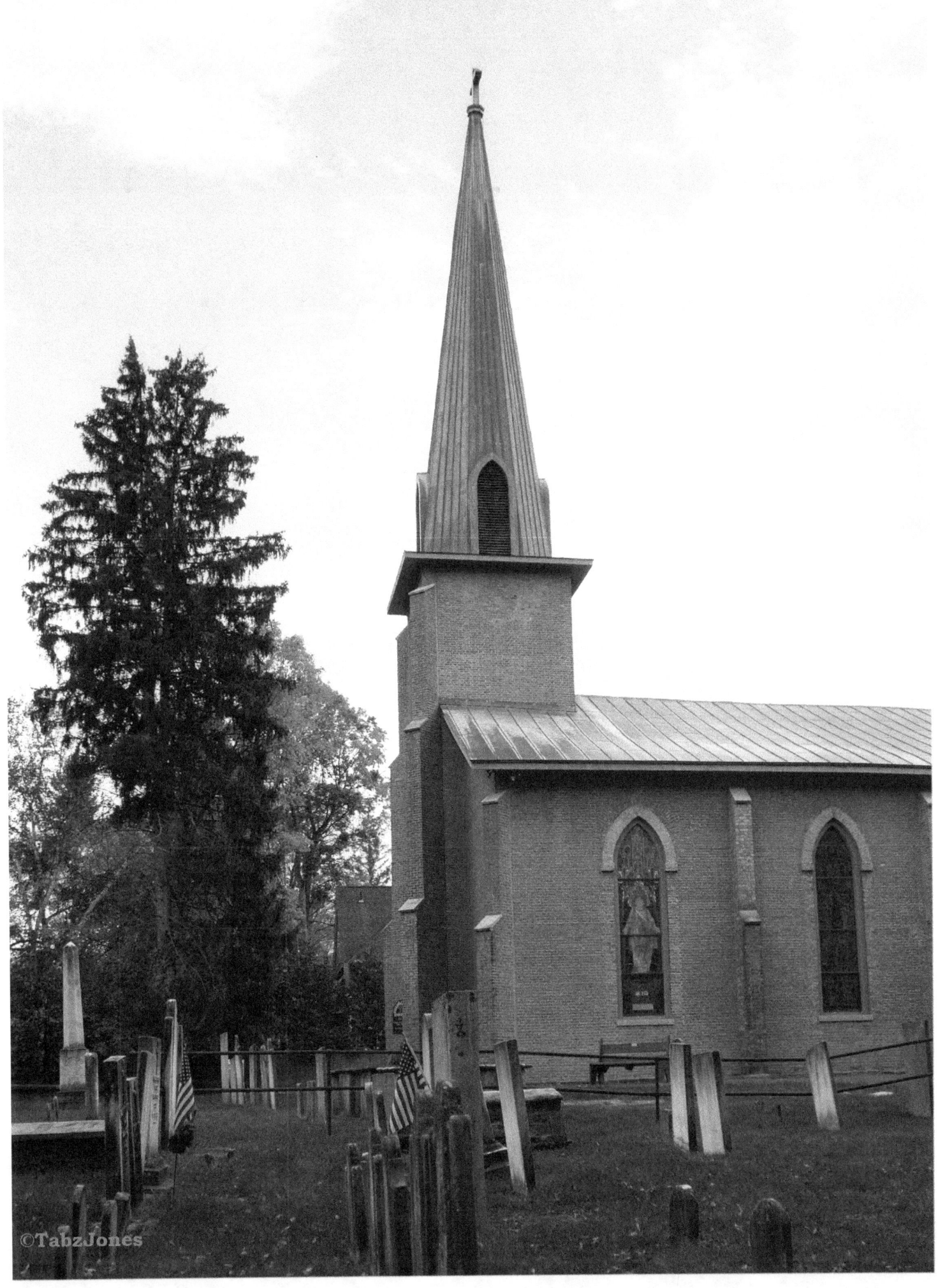
©TabzJones

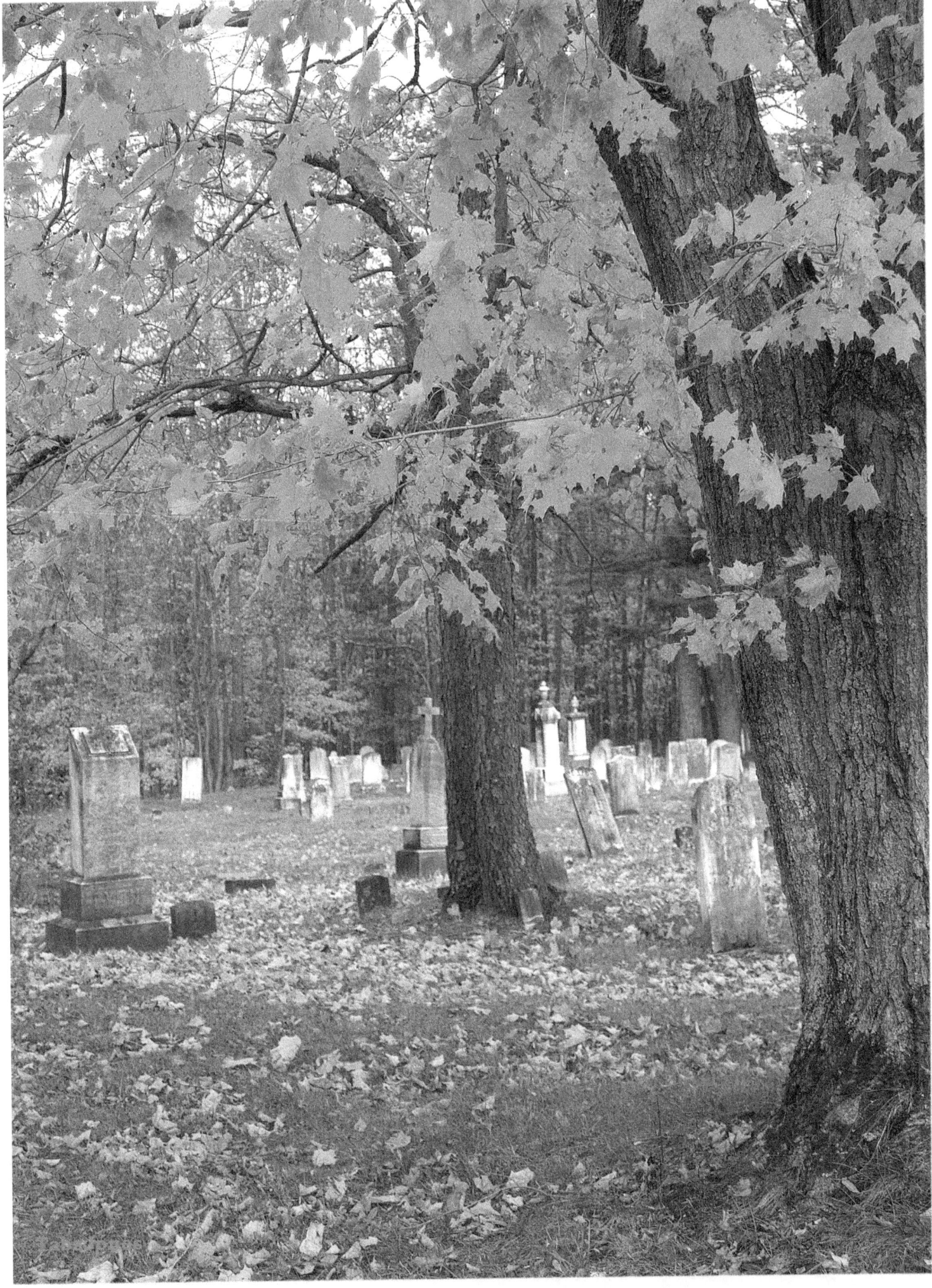

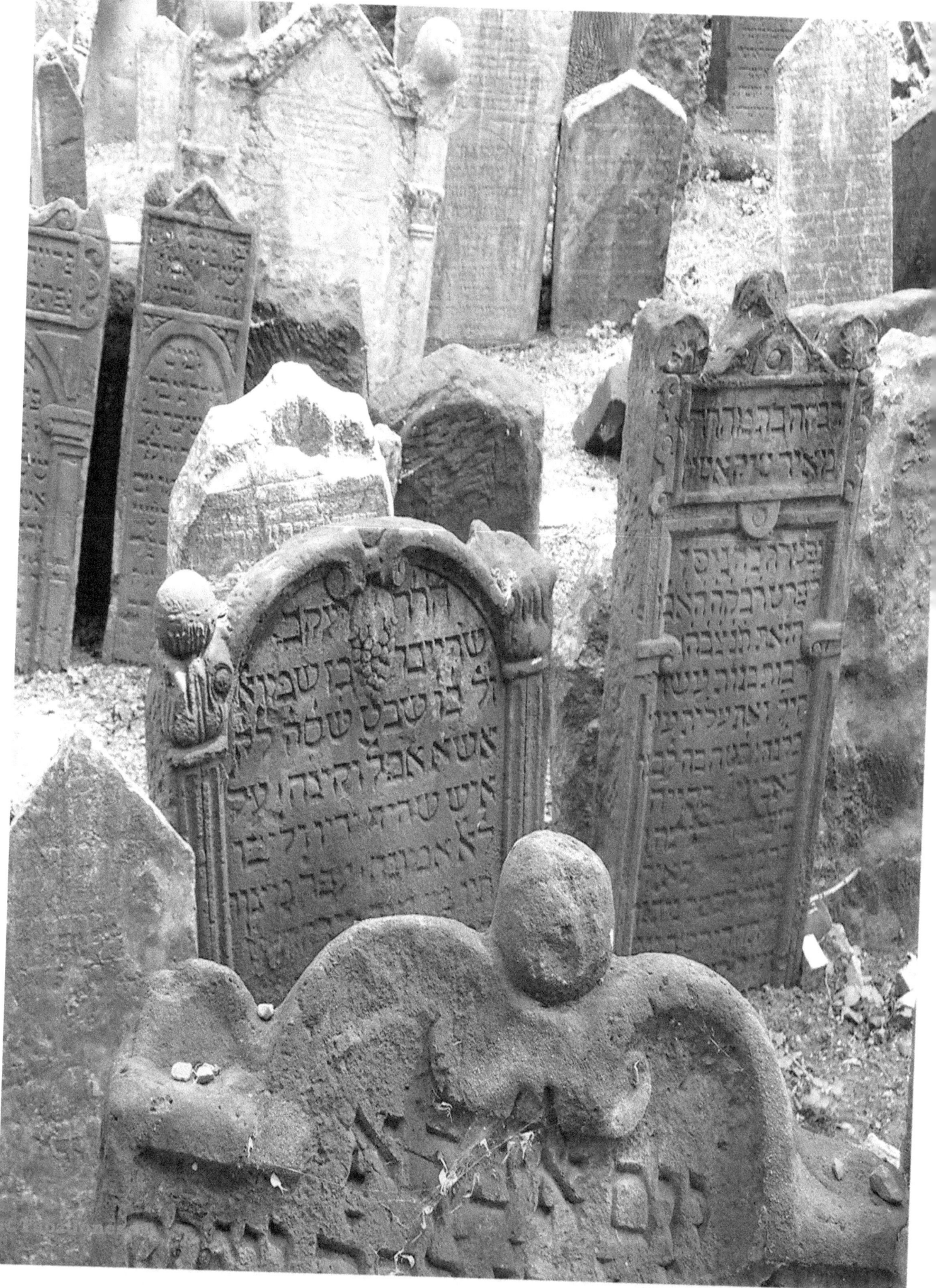

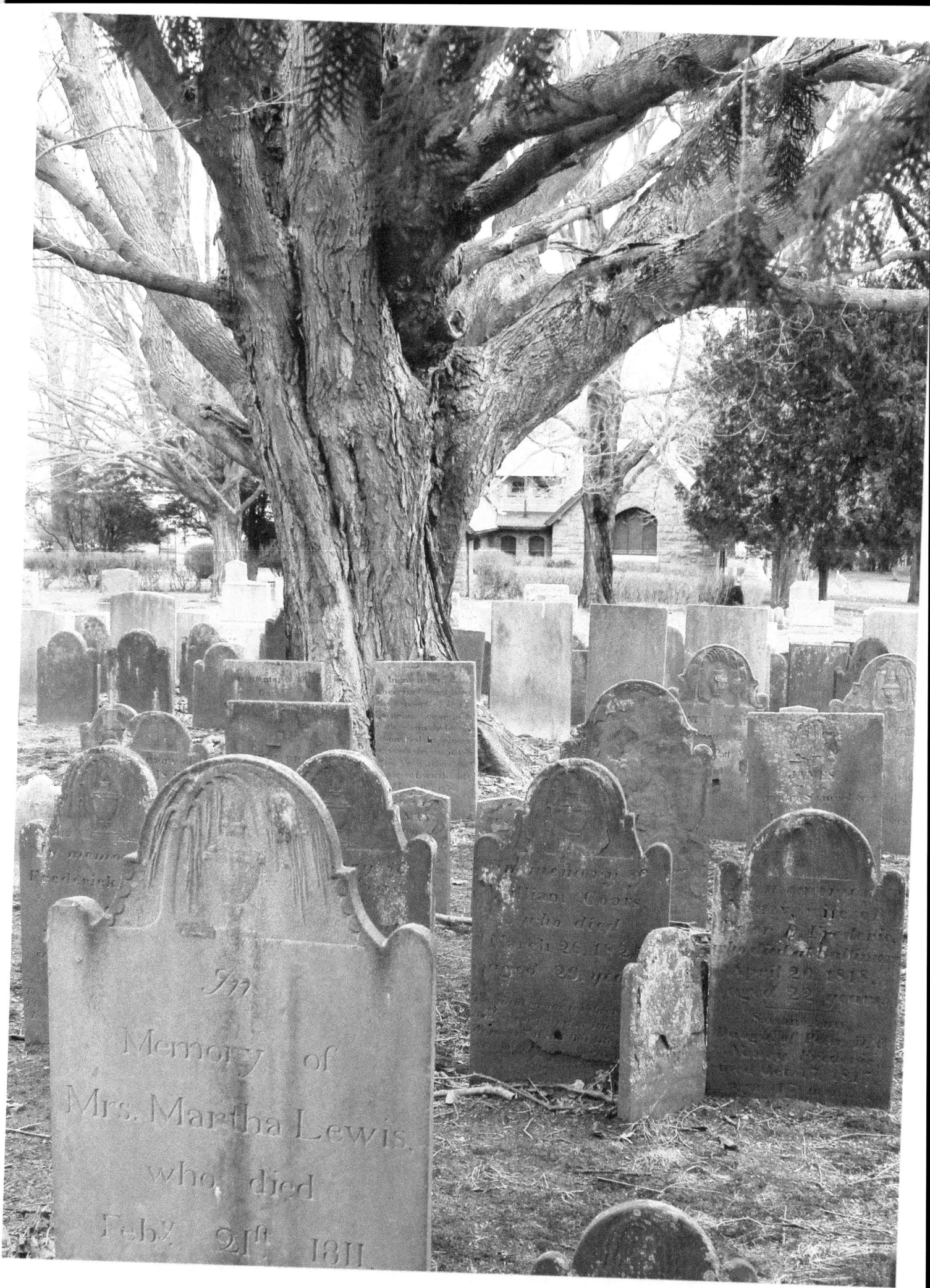

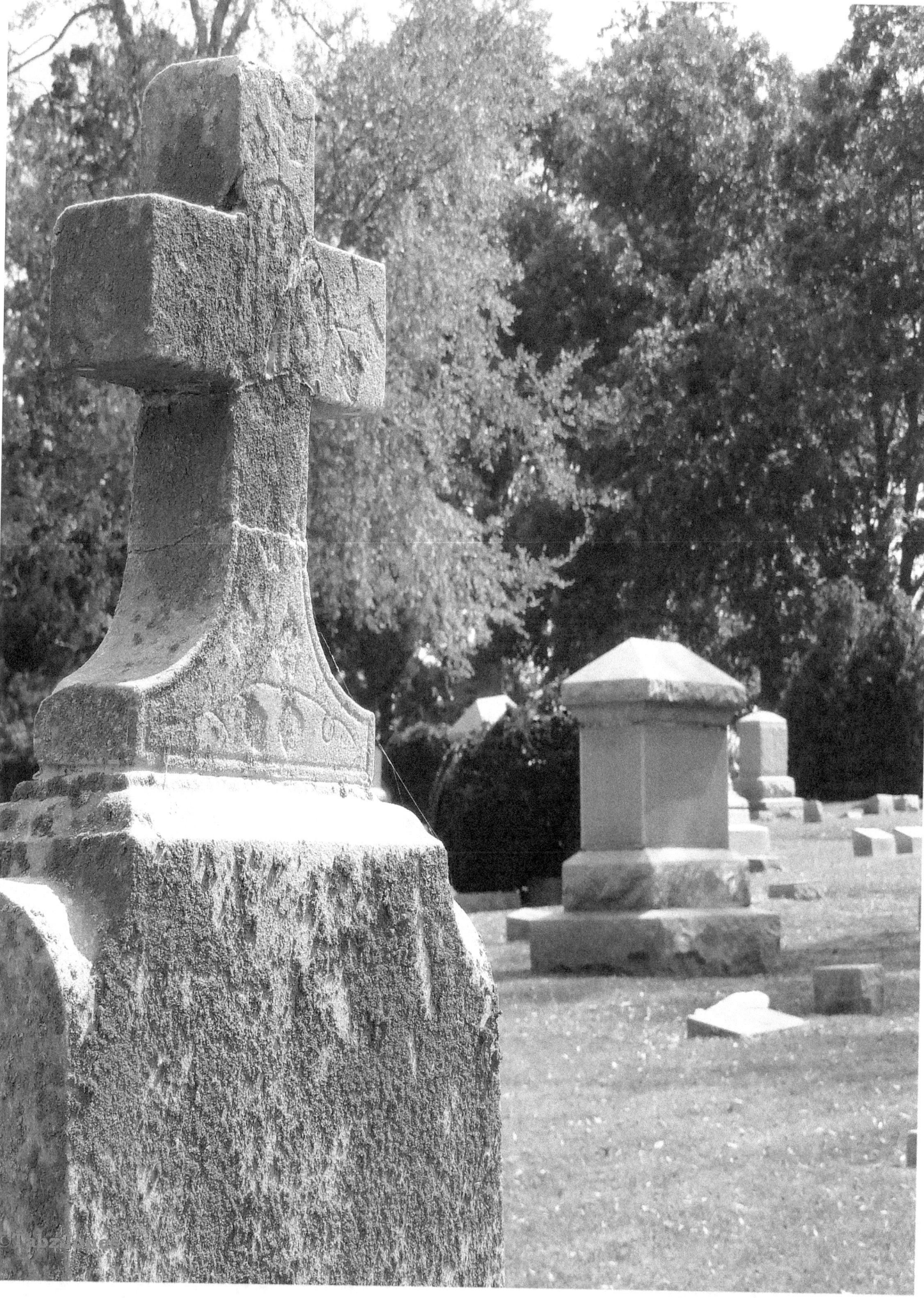

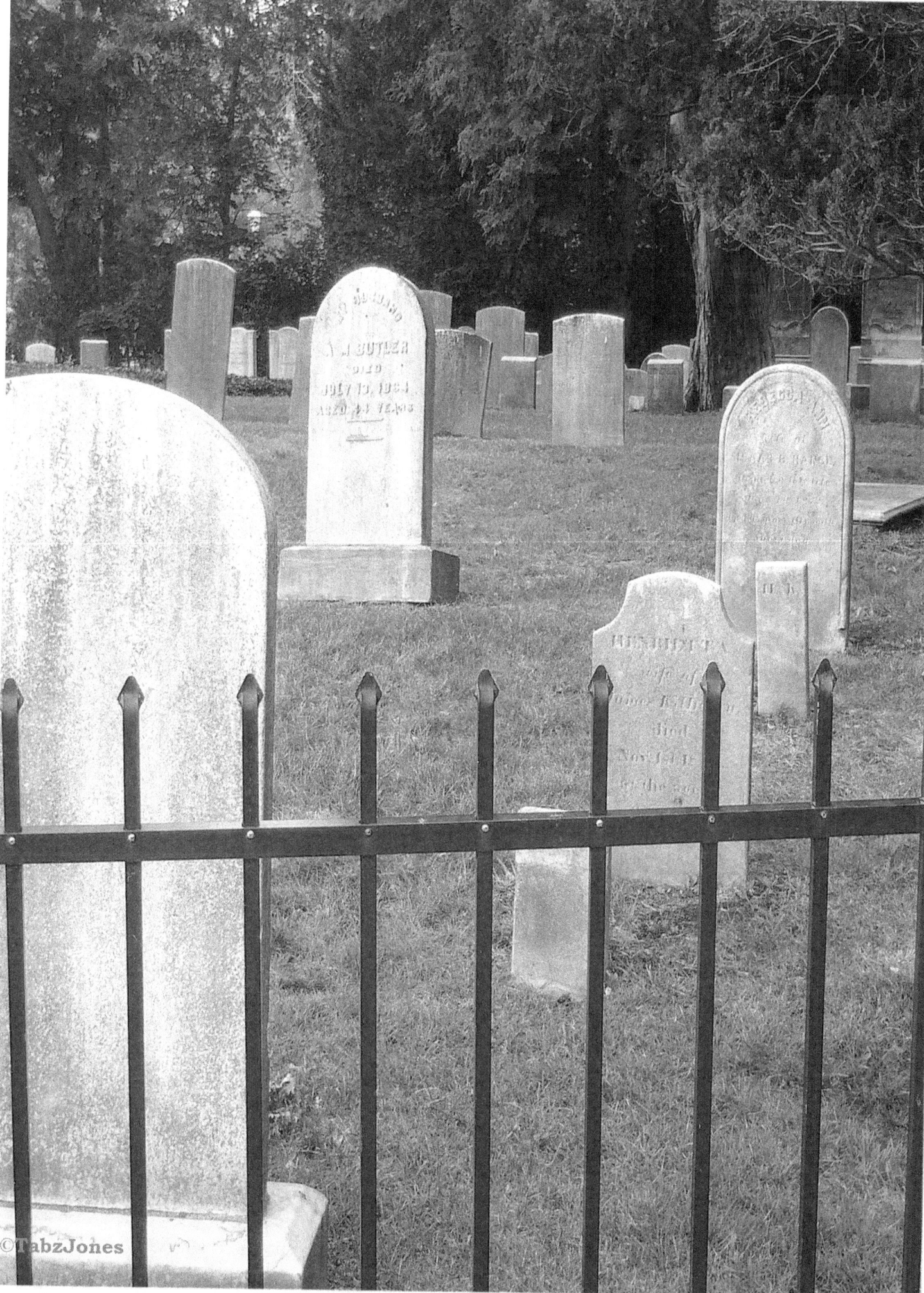

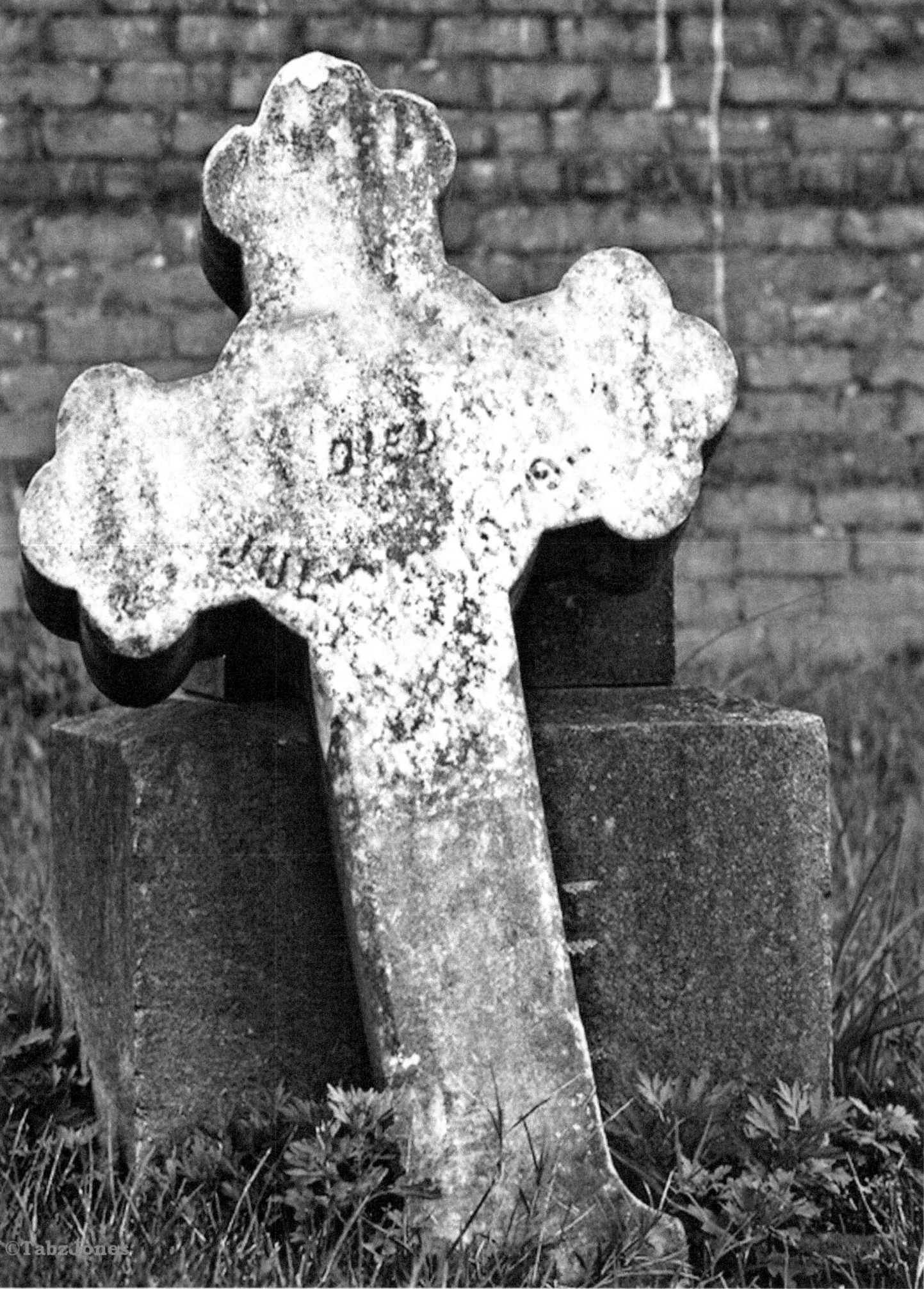

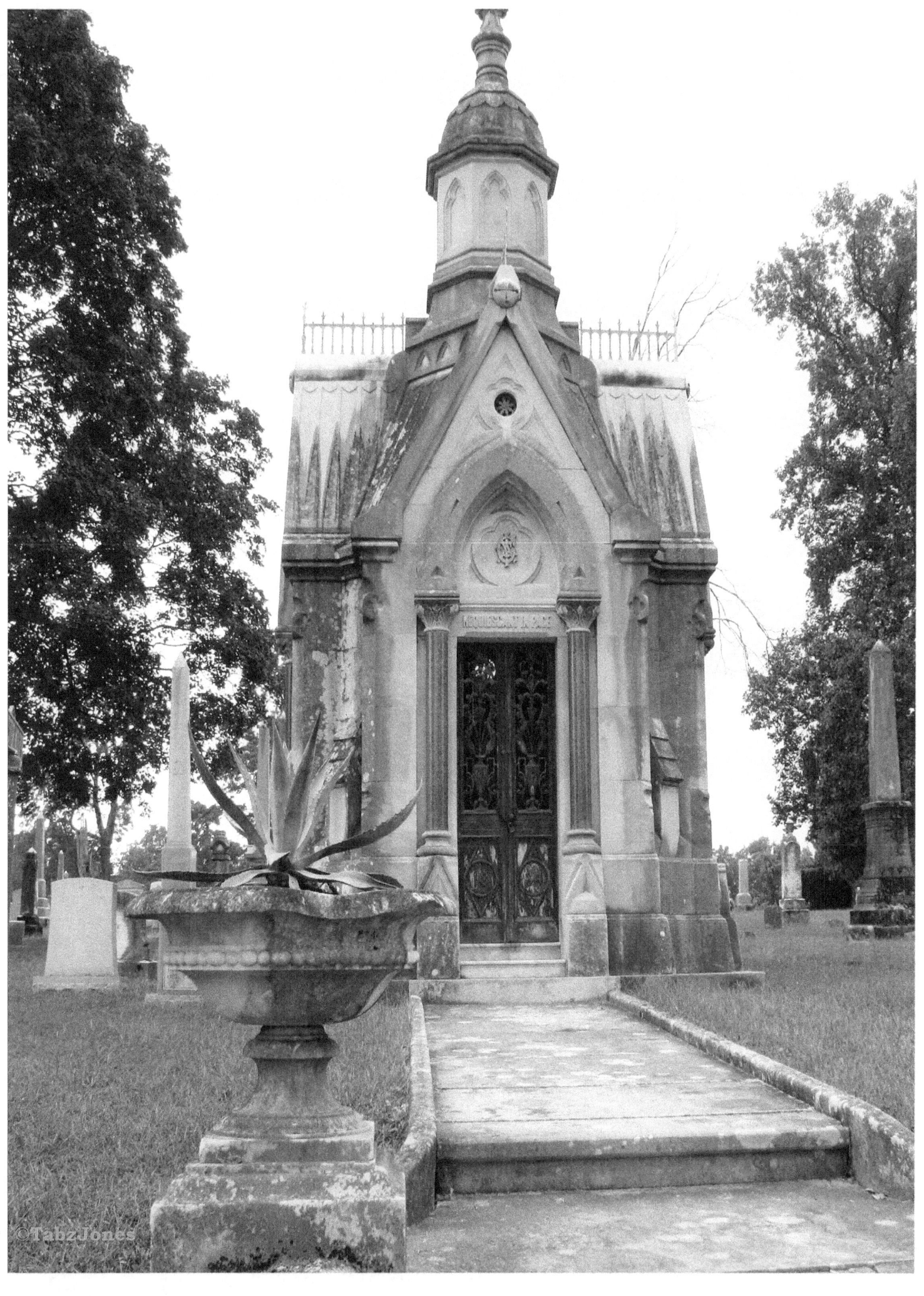

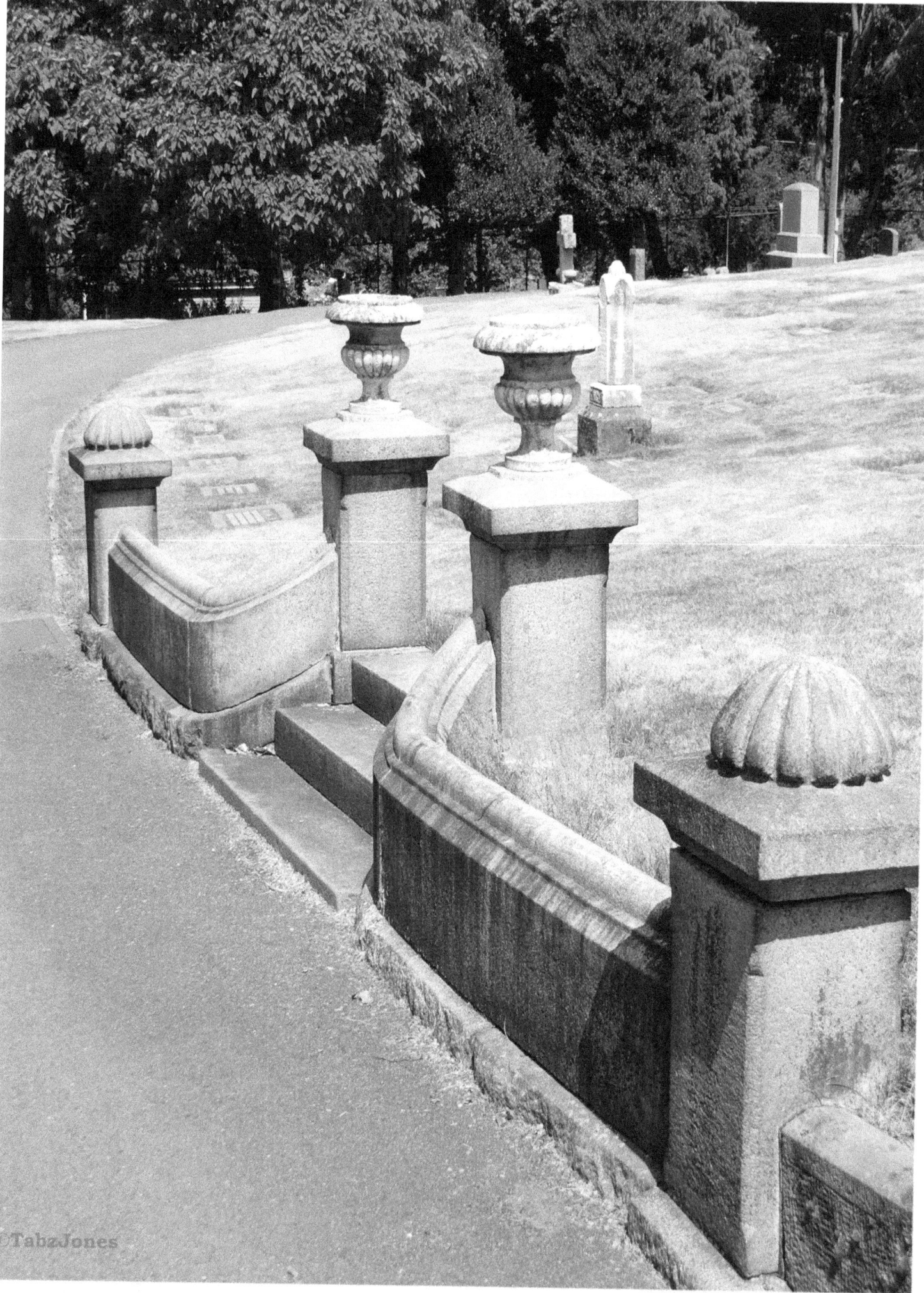

www.ingramcontent.com/pod-product-compliance
Lightning Source LLC
Chambersburg PA
CBHW080547190526
45169CB00007B/2669